The Strawberry Roan. — by Jim Bramlett

Will James in Reno Town. — by Jim Bramlett

"With his belly snappin' at his backbone,"
Bill waited for an Invite to Dinner. — By Jim Bramlett

Ride for the High Points

The Real Story of

WILL JAMES

Jim Bramlett

MOUNTAIN PRESS PUBLISHING COMPANY
MISSOULA 1987

The paper used in this publication meets the
minimum requirements of the American
National Standard for Permanence of Paper for
Printed Library Materials Z39.48 — 1984.

Library of Congress Cataloging-in-Publication Data

Bramlett, Jim.
  Ride for the high points.

  Bibliography: p.
  Includes index.
  1. James, Will, 1892-1942—Biography. 2. Authors,
American—20th century—Biography.
  3. Artists—United States—Biography. 4. Cowboys—United
States—Biography.
I. Title.
PS3519.A5298Z57   1987   813'.52 [B]   87-24755
ISBN 0-87842-214-5 (alk. paper)

Dedication

For Terry and Marcia Loebel

BOOKS BY WILL JAMES

Published by Charles Scribner's Sons

Cowboys North and South, 1924
The Drifting Cowboy, 1925
Smoky, The Cowhorse, 1926
Cow Country, 1927
Sand, 1929
Smoky Classic Edition, 1929
Lone Cowboy, 1930
Lone Cowboy Limited Edition, 1930
Sun Up, 1931
Big-Enough, 1931
Lone Cowboy Classic Edition, 1932
Uncle Bill, 1932
All In The Day's Riding, 1933
The Three Mustangers, 1933

Home Ranch, 1935
Young Cowboy, 1935
In The Saddle With Uncle Bill, 1935
Scorpion, 1936
Cowboy In The Making, 1937
Flint Spears, 1938
Look-See With Uncle Bill, 1938
The Will James Cowboy Book, 1938
The Dark Horse, 1939
Horses I Have Known, 1940
My First Horse, 1940
The American Cowboy, 1942
Will James Book Of Cowboy Stories, 1951

FOREWORD

Jim Bramlett is a long-time friend of mine, and I'm glad he wrote this book. I, too, grew up reading all the Will James books I could lay my hands on. We just read them and enjoyed them. We studied the drawings; and just about every kid with any "artistic leanings" copied them.

In those days we never questioned the thought that Will James was anything but a *cowboy* — and a very *talented* cowboy at that. He *had* to be, to write and draw like that, and to paint the kind of pictures he painted.

Then, as happens to anyone who gains a little acclaim, people began digging into his past. When this happened, little doubts began to appear, and a shroud of mystery clouded our hero. It looked like he was "dragging sagebrush behind his moccasins to cover up his tracks." Some writers went to great lengths to show that he had "feet of clay," but that happens often when anyone appears bigger-than-life. There are *builder-uppers* and *tearer-downers*, and both went to work on Will James.

Fortunately, the work he did stood the test of time, and outlived the man himself. He is still a hero today; not for who he was, but for what he did.

This isn't the only book on Will James, but I think it is the most complete. Jim back-trailed all he could, read everything about him that he could, and talked with and wrote to people who had known him, and has come up with an excellent book on Will James. He doesn't try to build up, or tear down; he tells all sides of the story. As you read, you will get to "know" Will James, and perhaps better understand him as a human being.

One thing more: Jim Bramlett is a talented individual himself. He has cowboyed, and he is a very capable western artist. And you will enjoy this book.

Sincerely,

Dick Spencer, Publisher
Western Horseman Magazine

Table of Contents

Will James, the cowboy's cowboy.

"There's more than plain riding and covering territory in this story – There's the sunshine, rains, blizzards and crosses of life on the range, – from the times I first remember – my raising amongst cowboys and trappers – my teachings from them, the open country and animals – More teachings after I'd growed up while always sitting on a horse – sowing my wild oats – reaping 'em – cutting my wisdom teeth on sharp edges of experience, and then finally lining out to ride for High Points–"

—Will James, *Lone Cowboy, My Life Story*,
Copyright © 1930 Charles Scribner's Sons;
copyright renewed 1961 Auguste Dufault.
Reprinted with the permission of
Charles Scribner's Sons.

x

Jim Bramlett on a hackamore colt at the historic Diamond Square Ranch of Fort Bragg, California, 1987.
— Photo by Eva Bramlett.

INTRODUCTION

IN THE SUMMER OF 1985 I checked out a couple of books from the county library that stood on the outskirts of a tiny ranching town in Nevada. In my usual style and quite by accident, I kept them longer than the allotted two-week period. A few days later I received a call from the librarian. She told me to return those books immediately. She informed me they were some of the most popular books in the library, and I was not allowed to keep them any longer.

One of the books was a Classic edition of Will James' *Lone Cowboy*. The book was printed in 1932 and was 53 years old. The other was a first edition of Will James' *Sand* that had been rebound. The cover may have been new, but those inside pages were printed in 1929 and were 56 years old. It's true that Nevada is a Western-oriented state, and books of the West are popular there, but nonetheless, I was impressed!

1

I had read most of the Will James books when I was a shirttail kid, and here I was reading them again. I enjoyed them as much as I did the first time, but I re-read them with a new sense of appreciation. During the days of my youth Will James was a distant hero, but as I've grown older he has become a real person to me. For some of us who live on the outskirts of civilization, ol' Bill's way of thinking continues to make a lot of sense. I thank God that areas remain where the West isn't completely tamed, places where bowlegged range riders can be seen "straddlin' down the road."

One of these cow towns in northern Nevada has a large custom-made saddle company. With pure enjoyment I browsed through their catalog, which featured specialized backaroo and horse equipment. On one page I found a photograph of a newly made but old-style buckaroo saddle accompanied by the following words:

> *"T.J." Symonds wrangles horses on the square skirted "Old Timer" for the I.L. Ranch. The I.L. Ranch at Tuscarora runs over six thousand head of cattle and is a nice place to work. Sam Collins, I.L. cowboss, says that one-half of the over one hundred horses they have in the caballada buck. He said that his crew very seldom "pulls" a horse and they pride themselves on being "forked." This is "slick fork country" and the entire crew is mounted on Capriola saddles, T.J.'s being the most authentic.*

— 1985 Capriola Saddle Catalog

Buckaroos of northern Nevada. Note spade bits, rawhide reins, 26-inch tapaderos, and war knots in horse's tail. (circa 1915) — Courtesy The Northeastern Nevada Museum, Elko.

2

The ad is in the language of the cow country and when translated means the IL (brand) ranch foreman is saying that fifty out of their one hundred head of riding horses will try to throw their riders when first saddled in the morning. He boasts that no rider in his crew will pull a horse's head up to stop it from bucking, because each man is proud of his riding ability. The foreman brags further that all of his crew is mounted on saddles that are in style on the ranges of northern Nevada. Those boys make little money, but they do take a lot of pride in their trade.

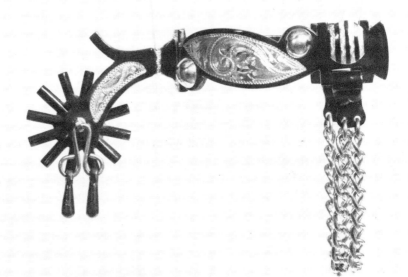

Silver-mounted spur with jingle-bobs, an old-time pattern. — Courtesy Capriolla Saddle Company.

The spirit of the Old West is an American heritage. It remains important for many of us and is kept alive by buckaroos, cowboys, horsepeople, artists, writers and the ageless books of a man who died years ago: Will James.

Ride For the High Points is not a complete biography of Will James. It is simply my attempt to capture vestiges of James' life in an era long past and to hold on a little longer to the nostalgia of a

3

period in the West when life was simpler and freer.

I did not go into much detail about Will James' demise to that ol' devil whiskey, for other authors have covered that period quite well. I wanted to capture him in his prime, when his genius was surfacing and he was contributing color and a historical record of the cowboy's West through his writings and art. It is a glimpse at what was actually going on in that blue range of hills over yonder during the teens and twenties of this century.

I interviewed Alice James Ross, Will James' ex-wife, two months before her death in May of 1985. We discussed Bill and his works in detail. She told me several interesting stories that will appear in the following chapters. An insight into the personality traits of Will James began to form through these meetings with Alice and also during interviews with Bill's sister-in-law, Agnes Dorish.

Clint and Donna Conradt (Bill's nephew and his wife) were especially helpful by contributing information and many rare, vintage photographs.

George 'Bim' Koenig (1911-1986), a lifetime rancher in the Topaz country of northern California, had a wealth of information on those notorious horse-breakers at the Rickey Land and Livestock Company in 1916.

Bevreley Haller shared colorful anecdotes with me about her hero and father, Curley Fletcher, who was a riding pardner of Bill's at the Rickey Ranch.

Abe Hays of the Arizona West Art Gallery in Scottsdale, Arizona, was my ace in the hole. Abe is a living authority on Will James, and his chronology of events in the life of the old cowboy/artist is completely accurate.

I have written the following pages from this information and also from Anthony Amaral's file, which was a pleasant surprise. Tireless in his efforts to track down information, Amaral put together a remarkable file on Will James over a period of six years. He probably did more to piece together the missing elements of James' life than anyone. After Amaral's death in 1982, his friend Nellie Laird donated the file to The Special Collections Department of the Uni-

Mounted on a good little gray horse, Will James drags a calf to the branding crew, where it will be branded, vaccinated, earmarked, and castrated if needed. —

versity Library at the University of Nevada, Reno.

I have taken several short stories and enlarged them to better illustrate the life and times of this colorful genius from the past, this man who called himself Will James. Occasionally I have written about his thoughts. These instances were created from information gained during conversations with Alice, who shared so many years with Bill.

Many others contributed special bits and pieces of information to complete my four years of research on Will James. He was pure Westerner, a man born to ride. I concluded the real story of Bill James could only be told by another cowboy.

Throughout the book I have used expressions a cowboy would use. Quite often cowboys will describe what happened to a horse or cow when describing something that was done to themselves. In 1942, S. Omar Barker explains why in an article entitled, "Sagebrush Spanish" that he wrote for *The New Mexico* magazine. "Unlettered men rely greatly upon comparisons to natural objects with which they are familiar to express their ideas and feelings. Mental images are a part of the life of a cowman. His comparisons are not only humorous, but fruity and unfaded."

As I think back to my youthful days, I remember men like Bill James, bowlegged gents with three-inch cuffs on their Levis rolling Bull Durham cigarettes (twirlys) and flipping the ashes into those cuffs as they waited nervously for the barber to "roach" off three months of hair so they could go out on the town and "howl at the moon!"

They would stroll out of that barber shop smelling like a whole field of flowers and with their faces sunburned from the middle of their foreheads to the bottom of their necks. With the exception of their hands, everything else was lily white, especially where the hair had been cropped three inches above their ears. All smiles from ear to ear, they were ready to take on everything the town had to offer. When the money was gone, along with their smiles, they took their provisions and their hangovers and headed back to some lonely camp in a world of horses and cows.

Ride For the High Points describes this kind of cowboy. Like most bowlegged men, Bill hated to walk if he could ride. He was a centaur, the sort of "feller" who would saddle an ol' pony and ride across the road to fetch the mail.

May you always ride a good horse.

Jim Bramlett
Fort Bragg, California, 1987

*Clay bust of Will James
by Jim Bramlett.*

Chapter I

PIED PIPER OF THE WEST

*"Can a man be a good cowboy and still turn out to be a writer
and artist? That question got as far as to reach me a couple of
times. My work had been looked at and criticized by a couple of
hombres that wore boots and Stetsons, but I don't know whether
they were cowboys or not, I never seen them. Anyway it was said
that a cowboy couldn't paint such pictures as what they was
looking at. Maybe it was meant as a compliment, but I didn't take
it that way. I took it they meant that the cowboy wasn't smart
enough to be able to paint like that and that's what I didn't like,
cause from my hair roots on down to the ground, I'm a cowboy,
and always will be no matter how much I paint, draw, or write."*

— Will James, *Nevada State Journal*
October 26, 1924

HIS DARK BROWN EYES were narrowed to mere slits as the slim youth slowly stalked across the abandoned quarry. He crouched, his hand hovering over the wooden handle of an old thirty-two caliber six-shooter. From behind him a voice yelled, "FUSIL!" (French for "shoot"). The youth's hand darted down and snatched the six-shooter from the holster with speed and dispatch. He cocked the hammer, and the round was "touched off" in the direction of a dirt bank, missing a tomato can by only a foot. Ernest felt good about his last shot. He had practiced that quick draw for the past hour, and his arm was getting tired, but he couldn't leave quite yet.

He gripped the revolver with both hands, cocked the hammer, held the front blade on the bottom of the pictured tomato, and fired. He drilled the red oval dead center from ten feet away. Buffalo Bill couldn't have done any better, he told himself.

Ernest emptied the pistol and turned to depart from the secret rendezvous place. His little brother, Auguste, ran out of the bushes and dutifully fell in behind him.

Many years later Auguste Dufault described those youthful days he spent with his adventurous brother. He admitted he was only amused by Ernest's attempts to become a quick-draw artist, but he was extremely proud of his brother's ability to draw with a pencil.

> Ernest knew how to draw as soon as he could hold a pencil, he had that perfect coordination which enabled him to translate on paper accurately whatever his mind had pictured. He was always scoffing at copying a subject. His mind could photograph anything, action or movement, and that photograph was the model on which he would draw. He would spend hours studying horses, cows, and dogs, staring at their movements, their eyes, expressions, the work of the muscles, the legs, the tails, ears, nostrils, etc. Then in the kitchen as he lay on the floor, flat on his belly, he would draw them on a piece of wrapping paper. As he could not see cowboy life in the making, he would imagine what it would be like.
>
> He had a great admirer, and that was me, and whatever he set

out to draw in his room I was always there to watch him, and he did not always like it, and you can understand for I was moving around and asking questions, which I understand now disturbed him quite a lot. So he complained to Mother, asking her to make me "git."

He had his subject so completely in his mind that I saw him several times start a drawing in a corner of a piece of paper, drawing sideways and putting in every character, subject, and detail until the full picture was finished when he had reached the opposite corner.

In Saint Hyacinthe, Province of Quebec, where for awhile my father owned the Hotel Union, he [Ernest] would draw all kinds of Western scenes on the plate glass mirrors behind the bar with a piece of soap. As I can remember, they were beauties and considered quite an attraction.

Brotherly love was an honest emotion on the face of the middle-aged man. His brown eyes were gentle as he went on to describe the never-forgotten boyhood days from long ago in eastern Canada:

Nine-year-old Ernest Nephtali Dufault sits by his father, Jean Dufault. His admiring brother, Auguste, is seated by his mother, Josephine. Standing are Ernest's sisters Eugenie (left) and Helene (right). (circa 1901) — Special Collections Department, University of Nevada Reno Library.

I have a family picture with Ernest in it, and we treasure it, as you can understand. He was about nine at the time. He looks pale, as he had recently recovered from a very serious accident which affected his health for the rest of his life. I think it was partly responsible for his death at such an early date.

Thinking it was milk, he drank from a container in the kitchen. It was actually pure lye in liquid form. Only the prompt intervention of Mother and the doctor saved his life.

After he left us we were in complete ignorance of his doings except for the fact that his lack of knowledge of the English language caused a lot of embarrassing situations in his dealings with employers in the West. An inner love for horses, though, helped him a lot, and his handling of them amounted to quite a gift.

Joseph Ernest Nephtali Dufault, who was later to change his name to Will James, was born at Saint Nazaire D'Acton, Province of Quebec, Canada, on June 6, 1892. When he left for the West he took only $10.00 and a bag of provisions. He left because he was fascinated by the stories of Buffalo Bill and Sitting Bull, because he was crazy about horses and the wide-open spaces, because he wanted to be a rider.

In 1907 he departed from his family in eastern Canada. The fifteen-year-old lad headed toward the plains and mountains of the provinces of Saskatchewan and Alberta. Without a backward glance, the youth walked bravely into his dreams of the West. His Canadian family saw him only three times afterward.

Will James was an adventurer and a desperado. Excitement followed him all his life. He went to extreme measures to escape defeat and to tell the world that his West and the cowboy life he wrote about and believed in was the only code he could live by.

Thirty-five years later, on September 8, 1942, in Billings, Montana, a will was filed five days after the cowboy artist's eventful life had come to an end. The will read in part:

"... IV. All the rest and residue of my said estate, whether real, personal or mixed, of which I shall die seized and possessed, or to which I shall be entitled at the time of my decease, I give devise and bequeath unto Ernest Dufault, 45 Saint Andrew Street, Ottawa Canada, he being the sole heir and survivor of my dear old friend, Old Beaupre, who raised me and acted as a father to me."

We now know that Ernest Dufault and Will James were one and the same, but who was Old Beaupre? The surviving brother, Auguste Dufault, answered this question from the witness stand in a court hearing on February 24, 1944, to settle the estate of the deceased cowboy.

That story of Old Beaupre is pure fiction, and this character was invented firstly to create more glamour around his [Ernest's] personality and autobiography, second to kind of explain that French accent that he took a long time to lose even when he had forgotten his French ... In his autobiography, the characters are ficticious, but quite a few episodes are true if you change the place and have the scene acted in eastern Canada and around his home. The mention of "Old Beaupre" in the fourth paragraph of his will was obviously put there to prevent suspicion on the part of anyone who might think Will James should leave the biggest part of his estate to anyone so far away, without that person being a close relative.

I understand how difficult it was for him to decide to write my name down on his will, as that would have aroused curiosity and while he was living to risk letting his true identity leak out, especially after he had written such a book as the *Lone Cowboy*. By writing Ernest, instead of Auguste, he might have thought that while living I could easily say that nobody by that name lived here and he most likely thought that it would be easy for me, after his death, to have the matter adjusted as common sense shows that the only sensible and reasonable solution to the problem is that in this case "Ernest Dufault" was for "Auguste Dufault."

A 15-year-old Will James with a "hungry loop" spread on the ground is ready to head south to pursue mustangs. Photo taken at a cow camp on Sage Creek in Alberta, Canada.

Bill, as he was known around the cow camps and to his friends, had lived a double life and for good reason. As a youth in Montana, when he was learning to become a professional cowboy and to speak English, the older cowboys teased him incessantly. To protect himself and to explain his broken jargon, he made up a story about himself, which he told around the ranches where he worked. In 1930 when his autobiography was published, this was the identical story Bill had written in its beginning chapters.

Bill admired the good riders he'd encountered on the big ranges, and he had created this story to impress them. The slim teenager wanted to be accepted as a cowhand, but life on an open range roundup is complicated and the rules of range etiquette are adhered to strictly.

At every roundup wagon the foreman or cowboss is in charge and all work revolves around him. The cook, if he's a good one, is second in importance. The top hands and the roughstring rider come next, followed by the general run of professional cowboys. The big ranches rounded out their crews with drifters or waddies (from the word wad or wadding, meaning someone to fill in). Horse wranglers and camp flunkies were at the end of the pecking order and were the starting jobs for boys wanting to become cowboys.

12

Will James' teenage years were spent riding the ranges of Montana, where he learned his cowboy trade from some top professionals. He went on to "earn his spurs" as a cowboy and bronc rider.

L.A. Huffman photos.

Lee Warren bridling a wild horse at Montana's Bow Gun Ranch in the early 1900s.

— Montana Historical Society, Helena.

Lee Warren gives the bronco a slicker lesson.

— Montana Historical Society, Helena.

13

"The Liars' Hour" at Montana's SH Ranch.
— Montana Historical Society, Helena.

A well-equipped camp at Montana's LU Bar Ranch where "Butch" the cook is baking bread in a sheet metal oven during the early 1900s.
— Montana Historical Society, Helena.

14

An important time of the day was the "liars hour," that brief interlude of relaxation after supper when the men were able to visit, tell stories, and have a few laughs. A good joke has always been the cowboy's staff of life, all the better if the men were laughing with you and not at you. On long rides the cowboy seldom had anyone to talk to other than his horse. So when a rider got a chance to visit, his tongue became "plumb frolicsome."

On the sweeping, moonlit prairie around a warm campfire, storytelling was whetted to a fine edge, which cut away those lonesome feelings and earned a newcomer his place in the comradeship of the bowlegged, leather-covered men. The stories were mostly fact. Cowmen know how to squeeze the juice from the American language, and instead of simply describing something, they paint colorful word pictures with pungent, salty phrases.

> *One of the inherent characteristics of the cowboy is exaggeration. Not only does he have a talent for telling tall tales, but he has a genius for exaggeration in ordinary conversation.*
>
> *Another pronounced trait is the pithy, yet robust humor which continually crops out in his speech. Struthers Burt writes, '. . .this closeness with nature makes the cowboy exceedingly witty. They are the wittiest Americans alive. Not wisecracking like the city man, but really witty.'*
>
> — Ramon F. Adams,
> *Western Words, A Dictionary of the American West*,
> University of Oklahoma Press
> Norman, Oklahoma, new edition, 1968.

Bill's teens and twenties were spent working on ranches, and he went on to "earn his spurs" as a bronc rider, a cowboy, and a storyteller. His writings were based on his and other cowboy's experiences. As with many dreamers and romanticists, Bill's stories were derived from a merging of truth and fiction. There's as much truth in his novels and short stories as there is fiction. There's as much fiction in his autobiography as there is truth. "I was born close to the sod," he wrote, "and if I could of seen far enough I could of glimpsed horses thru the flap of the tent on my first day while listening to the bellering of cattle and the ringing of my dad's spurs."

In *Lone Cowboy* Bill told the story of being born in a wagon in the Judith Basin of Montana. His father was a Texas cowboy and a drover, his mother a dark beauty of Californio bloodlines. Bill wrote that his father was fatally gored by a steer a few years later, and that after his death, Bill was entrusted to a grizzled, French Canadian trapper known as Old Beaupre. Bill called him Bopy.

Bill wrote an adventure-laden story of how he and Bopy travelled the wilderness trails north into the Peace and McKenzie River country of Canada. They set trap lines and lived in isolated cabins and dugouts. Snow averaged from six to ten feet deep, and the mercury dropped into the bulb and stayed there. It was a tough country. Bill gained his education from reading old catalogs and newspapers. He told how Bopy kept him supplied with pencils and paper for drawing.

He wrote that when the geese flew south in the fall he and Bopy would ride north, exchange their horses for snowshoes, and trap all winter. In the spring they would migrate south and ride into the Montana country for the summer. Footloose days began for Bill

An early Will James drawing. — Special Collections Department, University of Nevada Reno Library.

16

when Bopy was drowned in a swollen river and the lad was left to wander by himself.

Without a doubt, Bill experienced some of these adventures, maybe even sharing them with an Old Beaupre. His life was certainly a series of exciting events. In the early 1900s much of the United States and Canada was composed of huge, undeveloped expanses of country. Will James, the drifting cowboy, rode "smack dab" through the middle of it all. Bill ardently believed that a man who could leave civilization with his blankets and his bacon and make a living off the country need envy no other man.

In 1910 Bill made his first visit home to his Canadian family. Auguste had a good laugh as he described Bill's attempt to show off a little, cowboy fashion:

> The second day of his sojourn with us, he procured (I don't know how) a pinto bronc, saddled him, and started on a stroll throughout the city. As it was raining his horse slipped on the wet pavement in front of Viger Station — just imagine the scene — at that time the Montrealers had never seen a real cowboy otherwise than in storybooks and magazines. A crowd of quite a few, young and old, had been following him as best they could. He remounted and finally came home after playing havoc with the traffic and police. My parents did not know what to do, and it took two hours for the police to disperse the crowd. Ernest was swearing at the easterners calling them a bunch of ignorants who had never seen a thing!

Some writers have said Will James was a genius. Others have said he was a drunk. Many have said he was a drunken genius. Everyone who knew Bill admits that in his day he was a good cowboy and "one helluva" fine bronc rider. However, writers have neglected to record one simple fact: Bill was also very human. He had his share of talent, but like many folks he had his share of prejudices, ambition, and, always, compassion for his friends.

In 1922, after his close friend and benefactor Burton Twitchell was ordered to a hospital for an emergency operation, Twitchell received a long letter from Bill. "We sure wish you luck at the hospital," Bill wrote in the letter," . . .and that you come out stepping high. I wonder if the Big Boss would listen to a roughneck cowpuncher's prayer? Would he? Let me know."

On May 29th, 1934, a lonesome Bill, who was separated from his wife and drying out at a clinic in California after a long siege of heavy drinking, reached out to his brother-in-law and sister-in-law at his ranch in Montana. The letter began:

> Hi There — What in hell is the matter with you crowbaits that I don't get a word from any of you? Alice seems to be the big bug in getting word from the ranch and I'm not mentioned. Nobody seems to give a damn whether I'm afoot or worse and the good turns I done seem to be forgotten, and getting wild as I did seems to be all held against me instead. Of course I know that's not true, but doggone your lazy hides I like you all a plenty and I wish you wouldn't entirely forget this ornery sonofagun.

Joe De Yong, a protege of the great artist Charlie Russell, was a close friend of Bill's. He made the trip from his home in Santa Barbara to visit Bill in Hollywood whenever the cowboy was in town. De Yong wrote:

> James was beyond all doubt an exceptionally gifted person. Not only that, his ability in certain fields related to the arts did not have a chance — time rather — to become fully developed. On the other hand he was far more intelligent than many of his acquaintances could possibly understand, let alone give him credit for. His judgement in business affairs was the best of any of the small group of genuine cowboy artists of his day.
>
> While I have talked with various ones who were somewhat critical of James, mostly due to his continual drinking, I myself found him most friendly, patient and obliging. While I regretted the fact that he, in my opinion, did not make the most of his opportunities, and that his too-early death was the direct result of his not taking care of himself, he was at all times a good friend in whose judgement I had complete confidence.

The New York City firm of Charles Scribner's Sons published most of Will James' works, including *Lone Cowboy* and *Smoky The Cow Horse*. The publishers had Bill on a busy schedule that included lecturing at colleges. He also made trips to the larger rodeos and covered these events for the newspapers. He was hailed as the "numero uno" writer on rodeos, roundups, ranch life, cowboys, horses, and the entire Western scene.

Lean and tan, with deep-set, piercing brown eyes, he possessed a mop of black hair, aquiline features, bowed legs, a small waist, slightly hunched shoulders, and a mouth set in a firm, straight line. These are some of the Will James features that so impressed people. He was the idol of the juvenile world and a hero to thousands of adults. Bill modestly attributed his popularity with kids to the fact that his stories were based on fact. "You can't fool a kid," he stated. "They know when a thing's really so."

Smoky The Cow Horse blazed all the literary paths for Bill in 1927. When he gave the public *Lone Cowboy, My Life Story* in 1930, Bill's popularity soared to new heights. Reviews were extremely favorable, and all concerned enjoyed the rapid sales. But Bill had the proverbial "bear by the tail," and he was afraid to turn it loose. He knew he had made a mistake in writing the little story that he

A handsome Will James poses for the camera in Hollywood during the early 1920s.
— Courtesy Les Pons.

19

had told since boyhood. He worried about those fictionalized beginning chapters in *Lone Cowboy* because the critics were raving over the autobiography and they labled it "The Real Cowboy Saga."

Bill visited his Canadian family in 1925 and again in 1934. Auguste testified about these meetings in that same court hearing in Billings in 1944:

> When my brother Ernest visited us in Ottawa, he insisted that all drawings and letters which might reveal his true name be destroyed, and he was so insistent that we had to give him the drawings which we had at home, and he tore them in my presence. With regards to future letters, he repeatedly asked me to make a solemn promise that I would destroy them as soon as I had read them, so afraid was he that his true identity be found out in Billings.

On May 29th, 1961, while doing research for his book *Will James The Gilt Edged Cowboy*, Anthony Amaral received the following letter from a pal of Bill's, a renowned author and artist by the name of Ross Santee. It read in part:

> I liked Will James. I saw his first drawings when I was in cow camp. I met him in New York. Lee Townsend, a painter of horses, brought Will down to my joint when I was wintering

Flint Spears, *by Will James, published in 1938.*

20

there. When I told Bill he looked more like an Irish scholar than a cowpuncher his eyes clouded. "I've been hurt," he said. He looked like a man who'd been hurt. Then I asked him if he was the boy that Dave Reed, a cowboy I'd worked with in Arizona, had told me about; this cowboy worked with Dave in Nevada. I said, "Dave called you a little black devil,' said you drew pictures all over the place." Bill smiled; his whole face would light up when he smiled. He remembered Dave.

I saw him next at a rodeo in Chicago in '26, the Chamber of Commerce put it on big; they had writers there from all over the country. Bill and I were the only two that drew. He had more natural talent than any man I've ever known. He was doing a piece and a drawing for one of the papers; each time he'd ask me to go over it. He wrote in an old-fashion script with a fountain pen, he never made any changes, and he drew with the same pen.

Bill had a photographic mind. It was interesting to watch him work, he drew all over the page. At first the lines were meaningless, but they soon took form and the horse or steer, whatever he drew, would explode right off the page.

We all drank too much. When he drank, Bill was "muy coyote." He never talked pictures or artists. He mentioned Maynard Dixon, who once tried to help him; none of the old masters meant anything to Bill, nor did Bellows or Sloan, whom I admired tremendously. He had met Charlie Russell, admired his work. But Bill was off on his own. So mostly we talked horses and cows.

We were in Chicago three successive years, two weeks at a time. Eventually Bill told me about his hitch in the pen. When I kidded him about getting caught he didn't take it too well. We corresponded as long as he lived.

The first part of "Lone Cowboy," I think, is the finest thing he ever wrote. The fact that it was fiction and Bill thought it was fact never made any difference to me. Bill didn't know the difference between fact and fiction. He was awfully hard to pin down. He'd speak of "them southern countries" where he'd worked. One time I said, "goddamn it, states have names an' when a cowboy works for an outfit the brand is known!" I think that was when he first admitted to me he'd been on the dodge.

I liked his black an' whites much better than I did his oil paintings.

end of letter

In Will James' early life he was a shy, unassuming young man who enjoyed showing off with his bronc riding and picture drawing. Nevada had some houses that broadened a young man's education, and Bill eventually stopped blushing. He later became a trifle worldly.

In the summer of 1933 Bill went to Hollywood to work in the film adaptation of the book which he commonly referred to as the classic: *Smoky The Cow Horse.* He wore store-bought clothes to the studio but changed back to range clothes in his hotel room just before the entrance of a reporter from a large Los Angeles newspaper.

"How about staying down here and going into pictures," the reporter asked him," . . .and being an actor like Tom Mix?"

"I jest don't like cities, Bill replied. "One's same as another to me. I don't pay attention to which one it is. . . I don't like any of them. I like the country."

"Why do you wear cowboy clothes in a large hotel like this one?" the reporter asked as he tried to get a reaction from Bill.

"I wear these clothes for pajamas," Bill replied without cracking a smile. "The spurs keep me from sliding out of bed." The reporter's ensuing article ended with the following account:

> James has given up riding bucking horses, except now and then. His chief diversion is 'heavy roping,' which is to say roping heavy bulls.

> He is confident Fox is making a real picture in *Smoky*, and is enthusiastic over the work of Victor Jory, Irene Bentley and the very nearly human horse that plays the title role. When he and Miss Bentley parted following their first meeting, the charming young actress turned and said: Goodbye, Mr. James. . .

22

James didn't say a word for a moment. In evident admiration he looked after Miss Bentley. Then very definitely he replied: "Goodbye, Hell!"

During this stage of his life Bill was caught up in a whirlwind of activities. He had an 8,000-acre ranch to pay for, a responsibility to an admiring public, a demanding publisher who had advanced him a good deal of money, and a marriage that was in trouble. Everything was contingent upon his ability to produce, in words and drawings, pictures of a simple and healthy way of life that he, himself, would never again have the time to be a part of.

Underneath the complex facade of success was a lonely man, a man longing for simplicity in his life. Bill had a one-track mind,

Dressed for the city, Bill takes time out for a smoke and dreams of his ranch in Montana, The Rocking R. — Courtesy Clint and Donna Conradt, all rights reserved.

with thought patterns that could only survive in their own environment. When in cities attending to business, he was continuously homesick for the desert, the mountains, and livestock. When depressed he would invariably want to ride into the desert, where he could forget his problems. He felt humble and content where nature abounded.

In 1940, while visiting his friend Dick Dickson in Palm Springs, Bill was thumbing through a book written by an old-time cowboy, Bob Beverly, when he exclaimed, "This cowboy knows the same feeling that gets me." The paragraph read:

> The cowboy of the old west worked in a land that seemed to be grieving over something - a kind of sadness, loneliness in a deathly quiet. One not acquainted with the plains could not understand what effect it had on the mind. It produced a heartache and a sense of exile.
>
> — Hobo of the Rangeland,
> Bob Beverly, New Mexico, 1940

In his books Bill put into words his intense feeling for the wastelands, his excitement for a new horse. He actually was a participant in the saga of the West, not merely an onlooker.

Abe Hays holds one of his treasured antiques, a vintage pair of batwing chaps with the Rocking R brand displayed in brass studs. It is unknown if Will James wore these.
— Courtesy A.P. Hays.

24

Abe Hays quite aptly judged the success of the cowboy/artist/ writer in the following excerpt from his essay, The Art of Will James, in *Will James: The Spirit Of The Cowboy*, reprinted by permission from Nicolaysen Art Museum, copyright 1985.

Frederick Remington, having left his mark forever on American consciousness, would pass on. . . . Almost immediately he would be replaced by C.M. Russell, who occupied the public's attention until his own passing in October, 1926. The very same month James, with the publication of *Smoky*, would burst onto the scene and dominate Western consciousness with his art and literature for the next twenty-five years.

All three artists rejected Eastern ways, left formal schooling in their teens and found adventure in the West. Each became a successful writer although Russell's literary triumphs came late and were mostly regional. All three drank to excess, were eccentric at times, and became celebrities. Each influenced enormously other artists in their time and still do today. They were unique in that they totally dominated their eras by capturing public awareness and respect. They literally shaped public taste. Their like has not been seen again. . . .

. . . In this nation's finest of all periods, his [Will James'] work was praised and his books were successful. James achieved his ranking despite being completely unresponsive to the major emphasis placed by artists and writers on the more popular and commercial themes of shoot-'em-ups and shoot-'em-outs. He totally shunned gunfights, shootouts, barroom brawls or range wars. He felt they distorted and marred one's perception of the West and the cowboy. James' violence involved that between animal and man. . . . James liked to direct attention to the range horse and its reaction to the circumstances. In this perception James was aided by his marvelous love and understanding of animals, particularly horses.

Russell said of James: 'you know horses every way from the Ace.' Ross Santee wrote that James drew the range horse better than anyone else. The New York Times insisted that James did the best bucking horses.

—*Will James: The Spirit of the Cowboy*,
Nicolaysen Art Museum, Casper, Wyoming, 1985.

Bill's books had an uncanny effect on people's lives. They became chronicles of how a cowboy lived and worked. Readers looking for the West of Will James and resenting changes brought about by progress became disciples of Bill's thoughts and dreams.

Will James was a Pied Piper, not only because of his storytelling and exciting illustrations, but because he was believable to his public. He and his work were one and the same. Bill wrote about and drew himself; he actually was the Lone Cowboy.

The legend of Will James will not die as long as there are hard-riding buckaroos like Jay Dusard (western photographer) and Ian Tyson (Canadian singer/songwriter) to keep the flame ever burning. Jay Dusard wrote the following words about Will James and Ian Tyson.

> Will James drew horses that jumped off the pages of books right at you. Those drawings and the stories that went with them quite simply inflamed (some say corrupted) the imaginations of several generations of young males the world over.
>
> I grew up east of the West, achieving adolescence while hazing a big, red, throaty-baritone tractor down southern Illinois soybean rows. Will James provided my mind's eye with its conception of the Western landscape and its exotic denisons, both bi- and quadruped. Ian Tyson grew up west of the West, on

Horses I Have Known *by Will James, published in 1940.*

26

British Columbia's Vancouver Island, and was similarly afflicted by the James books. They were given to him by his English-born father, who had arrived in Calgary in 1906 at age nineteen, where he bought a saddle and a sixgun and spent the next three years cowboying on the rangelands of southern Alberta.

Thanks to Will James and certain other compulsions, Tyson and I both made our separate runs at riding rodeo bareback broncs. A half-dozen donated entry fees and their accompanying bonejarring, yet benign, buck-offs were sufficient to exorcise my delusions of forkedness. But Tyson really cowboyed-up, and kept a-hookin' it on down the road until a shattered ankle landed him in Calgary General Hospital. There he took up the infinitely saner art of guitar pickin'. For a man who didn't want his son to be a cowboy, Ian's dad was a poor judge of gift books.

Maybe it's just because of Will James that there's still cow outfits and working cowboys; certainly the range cattle business is pursued more for quality of life than for profit potential. But as the flame works its way down to ember size, up rides Ian Tyson with his Cowboyography and his silver-belly Resistol and fans the Hell out of it.

WILL JAMES
by Ian Tyson

When I was but a small boy
My father bought me many books
'bout the creatures of the river banks
And the sins of old sea cooks
But the ones I never left behind
With the old forgotten games
Were the tales of wild and windy slopes
By the man they call Will James

The living of his cowboy dreams
Or so it seemed to me
The perfect combination
Of riding high and being free

27

His heroes were his horses
And he drew them clear and true
On every page they'd come alive
And jump straight out at you

His race towards the sunset
Was the high and lonesome kind
Like a coyote always looking back
He left no tracks behind
So I've memorized those pictures boys
They're still the very best
If whiskey was his mistress
His true love was the west

I remember up on Dead Man Creek
Back twenty years or more
I hired on to breaking colts
Which I'd never done before
A city kid I asked myself
Now "What would Will James do?"
And you know it was the damndest thing
But it kind of got me through

— From the 1984 album, IAN TYSON
by Ian Tyson

28

The big, round corral at the Ricky Cattle Company was the scene of many battles between man and horse. Here Bill "sticks like a postage stamp" on a black outlaw. —

Chapter II

THE DRIFTING COWBOY

"I lived in San Francisco for a spell and tried to get interested in art schools, but I'd always find myself drawing bucking horses and wall-eyed steers instead of trying to draw the model before me. It was there I learned I could never copy. I never sketched from nature or life, and what I drew is what I seen and felt while looking thru a horse's ears . . . my schooling was on a horse and looking at old magazines that was scattered around the cow camps. My first writing I'd print as I'd see it in saddle catalogs and I never went to a school house, only maybe to dance."

— Will James, *Nevada State Journal*
October 26, 1924

Harry E. Webb (1888 - 1984), who once rode with Buffalo Bill's Wild West show, had been a renowned cowboy, trapper, actor, and author. The 96-year-old Webb was named to the National Cowboy Hall of Fame in April, 1984. He knew of Will James when Bill was chasing mustangs in eastern Nevada. "When I first heard about the to-be-famous author, he was running mustangs in Pine Valley," Webb wrote. "At that time Will James was just another name to us Pine Valley folks, and although he had run afoul of the law, several such cases were then being disposed of in various courts so the incident was quickly forgotten.

"Some years later I began reading stories by a Will James, Montana writer, and then discovered that this author and Will James, the Pole Creek mustanger, were one and the same."

. . .

Nevada mustangs "burning the breeze." — Courtesy Bureau of Land Management

The wild mustang paced nervously as he circled his little bunch of mares. A breeze whipped the long, flowing mane around his handsome head as he tested the wind for some telltale sign of danger. Eyes blazing, little fox-like ears working back and forth, thin nostrils open wide, the black stallion was as wild and free as an eagle in flight.

The stallion heard a faint sound downwind and advanced to investigate. Halting to check the wind and then trotting forward, he circled the edge of a deep arroyo. As he picked his way through the sagebrush his neck was arched and his little feet hardly seemed to touch the ground, creating a picture of grace and power as he pranced back to his herd.

Two brown eyes in a grinning cowboy's face peered through the sagebrush as the man lay on his belly to watch the mustang. The black-haired cowboy felt a yearning for this horse, wanting to touch his silky hide and ride him out across the desert.

Bill James slid down a sloping bank to the floor of the arroyo. He had a plan.

As he clamped his Stetson tight on his head, he looked at his two pards, Tom Hall and Al Thatcher, sitting on their horses and holding his saddle pony by the McCarty lead rope.

"Boys," Bill whispered, "I'm gonna stay with the black 'till I catch him or 'till hell freezes over." He pulled his cinches tight and mounted his horse. After building a loop in his rope, he and his pardners were ready to give chase.

Crouching low in the saddle, Bill took the lead, walking his horse up the draw. The sounds of the horses' footsteps were muffled in deep sand. Arriving at a small tree Bill had spotted as a marker, he turned and nodded. The riders spurred up and over the bank at full speed.

The mustang herd stood in shocked surprise for a brief instant and then whirled as one, racing across the sage-covered flat. As the mustangs lined out at a dead run, they were a wonderful sight to see. Their long manes and tails streamed out behind them as powerful hind legs drove them across the desert.

At first the black stallion cast back and forth in the gap between the running herd and its pursuers. But when the cowboys began to gain on them, the stud accelerated ahead, weaving his way through the running horses.

There were several branded mares in this herd, and as they raced across the flat the fleeing horses merged with others that were branded. This was according to plan, for the mustangers decided their chances were better to corral these mustangs if the tamer, branded horses could lead the wild ones into their trap.

The wild horses race down a long, rocky ridge. —

Racing down a long, rocky ridge with timbered draws on both sides the lead horses suddenly swerved to the right, the older mares and colts plunging into the draw behind them. The black stallion quit the bunch at this point and, tail in the air, put on a show of speed that carried him through the left draw, down a big flat toward the breaks along Pole Creek.

Hall and Thatcher stayed with the main bunch, but Bill lined out behind the stud horse. The black raced along at breakneck speed over hills and through arroyos, and behind him came Bill, his horse gradually losing ground.

Bill worried that he would lose this race when he saw the black stallion go over a rise and disappear. He urged his tiring horse to the spot where he had last seen the stallion and then pulled the gelding to a stop. The terrain had dropped off rapidly, and he could see the black horse had lost its footing and was tumbling head over heels down the steep slope. Below the horse was a grove of cottonwoods, chokecherry trees, and brush bordering the creek.

Avoiding the dropoff, Bill spurred his horse to a point where he could slide the animal down on its hindquarters. In a cloud of dust he reached the bottom and, glancing to his left, spotted the black struggling to its feet. Bill charged toward the stallion. The wild horse outdistanced the rider to the creek bank, but it balked at the water's edge. This gave Bill a chance to close the gap and get into roping range. The stallion leaped into the brown run-off water, and the rider spurred his mount into its wake. As the horse climbed out the far bank, Bill fit a loop around that trim, black neck.

Bill was always a hard and fast roper, his rope tied on to the saddle horn, and now there was a thousand-pound black stallion fighting on the other end of it. His bay cowpony had a lot of heart, and it pulled the black around until the wild one choked down and fell over on its side. Bill dismounted in a flash. He wrapped his reins around the rope so his horse would face the black, then he ran over to sit on the mustang's neck. Rapidly he tied the rope into a halter, then mounted his horse as the gasping stud struggled to its feet.

The stallion propped all four legs and sulked. Bill's saddle horse dug in and dragged the stud to a chokecherry tree. The cowboy quickly rode a couple of turns around the tree, and dismounted to tie the rope off.

Bill backed off and stripped his rigging from the sweaty back of his tired saddle horse. While the lathered-up bay cooled, Bill reared back on his heels and rolled himself a Bull Durham cigarette. He touched a match to the twirly as his eyes took in all the good points of that black mustang. Bill felt mighty proud of himself for having caught such an animal.

When the bay gelding was cool and breathing normally, Bill saddled up and headed for help. He wound his way out of the creek bottom and onto the flat where he had last seen his two partners. He cut the tracks of two sets of shod hooves mixed with many unshod hooves and followed the easy trail for five miles along a canyon. A cloud of dust indicated he was close to Thatchers Canyon.

The scene he rode into was western and alive. Thatcher and Hall had succeeded in capturing most of the horses in a blind corral. They were busy cutting out the branded stock when Bill rode in.

"I got that stud," he enthused, "and is he a beauty!"

"Well, where is he?" Thatcher asked. "Did you lose him or find out he was branded and turn him loose?"

"Neither," Will said. "Drug him till my horse couldn't haul him any farther, so I tied him to a chokecherry tree and came in for help." Near dark, an hour later, the three had returned on fresh mounts only to find the stallion gone.

"Christ, Will," Hall said, "you never should have left him! He's busted your riata and hightailed it."

A corral full of wild ones.

34

"Wait a minute," James said. "This rope's been cut! I know damn well a thousand-pound horse couldn't break it!" On examining the area they found tracks showing where two riders had been skidding and hazing the stallion along.

"We can't do nothin' tonight," Hall said, "but come morning we'll track 'em to hell and back if necessary and get your horse or somebody's scalp."

Following the tracks to the Raines' Hat Ranch, the three saw the stallion in the round corral with a fresh Hat brand on him. As they sat their horses, Jim Raines and two of his sons came out of the house and hurried to the corral.

"Listen, you guys!" Hall demanded. "Get in that corral and vent that brand you stuck on our horse and be damn quick about it!"

"What you mean, *your horse*?" one of the Raines said. "We came along and that horse broke loose and after chasing him a mile we managed to rope him. He was a gone gosling as far as you're concerned. And since we roped him, he's ours."

"Like hell he broke loose!" Hall shouted. "Look at that fellow's riata there. A city dude could see that's the work of a knife!"

"Well," Jim Raines said, "the boys say they roped him and that's good enough for me. So what you go'nta do about it?"

"I'll show you what I'll do about it," Hall said, unholstering his Colt. "You're venting that iron or you'll never live to get any use out of that horse!"

"Oh, to hell with 'em, Tom," James said, as he grabbed Hall's arm. "Let 'em have the horse. We don't want a killing over a mustang! These lousy thieves are welcome to him as far as I'm concerned."

"It's your horse, Will," Hall said, calming down. Addressing the senior Raines, he shouted, "All right, Jim, you birds can have the horse but I'll make him the most expensive damned mustang you ever latched onto!"

— Harry E. Webb, "Will James and the Rustler,"
Nevada Magazine, July/August, 1984.

THE THREE MUSTANGEERS

The Three Mustangers *by Will James, published in 1933.*

By WILL JAMES

Tom Hall lived up to his word. He butchered many steers that wore the Hat brand, and sold the meat to a nearby mining camp. This spooked the mild-mannered Bill, who immediately made plans to leave and try to get a job on the McGill ranch near Ely, Nevada. He told Thatcher it was time to "vamoose while the gittin' was good." Thatcher said that made good sense, for he too was afraid Hall would land them all in the hoosegow.

Hall left that part of the country not long after Bill, but Hall's daring, hotheaded acts were much talked about after his departure.

Months later a neighboring rancher, Tom Jewell, told about the adventures of the Pole Creek mustangers to a new bronc rider for the Hat outfit; a ranahan by the name of Harry Webb.

> When Jewell finished the story, I [Webb] said, "Well, we've got to admire Hall's nerve even if we do have to damn his judgement. I've heard a lot about him, and it's a wonder he wasn't slapped in jail long ago. Raines isn't one to take such open-handed butchering and do nothing about it."
>
> "Scairt, that's why!" Jewell said. "Same as ol' Joe Dean was when Tom was butcherin' J.D. stuff. But Hall's probably in jail

36

somewhere because I read in the paper where they finally got his partner up for cattle stealin down . . ."

"Who's this partner you just mentioned!" I cut in.

"Feller by the name of Will James," Jewell supplied. "Him and Tom was mustangin' up around Pole Creek. But I see in the *Eureka Sentinel* they got James and some other feller for stealin' cattle by the carload."

To me, this was bad news. Although I didn't know Will James from Adam's Off Ox, I had a deep admiration for him just from what Thatcher had told me. I especially recalled Thatcher saying, "Funny thing about James. He always had a notebook jotting down things. Maybe it'd be some remark by a miner or a cowpuncher or the Chinese cook over at the Dean Ranch. Made no difference, down it'd go in that book."

Now as we look at Will James' classics, we can see that while he was running mustangs he was laying the foundation for a writing career. Perhaps *Smoky* was beginning to jell right there at Al Thatcher's. I asked Al if he had heard the news about Will James, as related by Jewell. "Bunk!" Al said. "I don't believe a damn word of it! He was one of the finest, straight-from-the-shoulder boys I ever met and I won't believe it until I get one of old Skillman's *Sentinels* and read it. Won't, by God, believe it then!"

— Harry E. Webb, "Will James and the Rustler,"
Nevada Magazine, July/August, 1984.

In 1915 Will James was twenty-two years old. His Nevada State Prison record shows that he weighed 135 pounds, was five feet, eight

The courthouse of White Pine County, Ely, Nevada.
(circa 1908) — Nevada Historical Society, Reno.

and three-quarters inches tall in his bare feet, and wore a six-and-a-half size boot. Bill was always proud that he had the small feet of a rider. But he wasn't very proud of himself on January 25th of that year as Sheriff Crain led him into the justice courtroom at Ely, Nevada. It appeared to Bill that half the residents of the county were there to witness his trial.

He looked longingly out of frost-covered windows at a blue line of mountains. Many years later Bill told his wife Alice that he had felt very small in that courtroom as he waited for his trial to begin. As the trial progressed, and throughout the months following, he often recalled the snowballing events leading up to his arrest and wondered at how quickly they had changed his circumstances. Even years later, Bill's stories relied heavily on these recollections.

At that moment, however, his only thoughts were wishing he was on a good saddle horse and hightailing it toward those hills on this crisp winter day. Bill was brought back to reality by the arrival of Judge Edwards. Soon the district attorney, Anthony Jurich, called his key witness for the state, Richard Swallow, to the stand. The following colorful dialogue is taken from the court reporter's transcript of the Justice's Court of Ely Township No. 1, of the county of White Pine, State of Nevada.

Question: "What is your full name, please?"

Answer: "Richard T. Swallow."

Question: "Where do you reside?"

Answer: "Shoshone, Nevada."

Question: "What county?"

Answer: "White Pine County."

Question: "You have been there for some time, haven't you?"

Answer: "Yes sir, born and raised there."

Question: "You are engaged in what business?"

Answer: "Stock business, and ranching."

Question: "Who is engaged in that business with you?"

Answer: "My brother, Ray G. Swallow."

Question: "You and your brother own a lot of cattle, do you?"

Answer: "Yes, sir."

Question: "Where do these cattle range? In and about Shoshone, in that country?"

Answer: "Yes, sir, in different directions, sometimes within twenty miles of the ranch in every direction."

Question: "All in White Pine County?"

Answer: "Well, sometimes in Lincoln County."

Question: "Did you miss thirty-one head of cattle, Mr. Swallow?"

Answer: "No sir, we didn't at that time, we hadn't missed them."

Question: "Did you miss them at any time?

Answer: "Yes, sir, we missed them later, along after we found out they were gone. Although we had received word they were missing before we drove that part of the ranch."

Question: "Did you see these cattle afterwards?"

Answer: "Yes, sir."

Question: "Where did you see them?"

Answer: "Ray, Colorado."

Question: "How many were there?"

Answer: "Thirty-one head."

Question: "Whose cattle were they?"

Answer: "They were ours."

Question: "How did you know?"

Answer: "By the ear marks and brands."

Question: "Did you examine them all?"

Answer: "Yes, sir, they had them all in a corral."

Question: "Did you sell those cattle?"

Answer: "Afterwards, yes, sir."

Question: "That is after they were there."
(Ray, Colorado)

Answer: "Yes, sir."

Question: "How did those cattle get there, if
you know?"

Answer: "They were driven . . ."

Route of rustlers, in the Snake Creek Range south of Sacramento Pass in White Pine County, Nevada. Will James drove his stolen cattle around the south end, at far right of picture, to get them into Utah. — Special Collections Department, University of Nevada Reno Library.

Bill thought back to that grueling ten days and nights: driving cows through the night's chill, holing up all day without much food, and afraid to build a fire to cook what little he had. The District Attorney's voice brought him back again.

Question: "Did you talk to this defendant, Mr. Swallow?"

Answer: "Yes, sir."

Question: "About when, if you remember?"

Answer: "About the day before Thanksgiving."

Question: "That is in November, 1914?"

Answer: "Yes, sir."

Question: "Where did you talk to him?"

Answer: "Here in the Court House in the Sheriff's Office."

Question: "Who was present?"

Answer: "There was Mr. Crain, and Mr. Millick, the deputy."

Question: "Did the other parties who were present have anything to say?"

Answer: "Some."

Question: "What was said by the defendant at this time?"

Mr. Lockhart: "Now just a moment, - was any promise made to the defendant at that time, Mr. Swallow?"

Answer: "No, sir."

Mr. Lockhart: "Was any inducement held out to him to say anthing to you?"

Answer: "No, sir."

Mr. Lockhart: "How did this conversation come to take place?"

Answer:	"He was just brought out of the jail into the office - I wished to speak to him for a minute or two."
Mr. Lockhart:	"Were any threats made at that time?"
Answer:	"Not that I know of."
Question:	"Now, what did the defendant say?"

Bill thought back to how he and Lew Hackbury were just riding along when the little bunch of cattle began to move out ahead of them. They joked back and forth about how they should rustle them and sell them. They joked some more about all the things they could buy with the money. Then Lew began to get serious and called Bill's attention to the lack of footprints of shod horses around, which indicated the cattle hadn't been checked on for awhile.

Answer:	"Why, we spoke about how they left the Reardon ranch over there."
Question:	"Who left Jim Reardon's ranch?"
Answer:	"This gentleman and Mr. Hackbury."
Question:	"The defendant and Mr. Hackbury?"
Answer:	"Yes, sir."
Question:	"What else did he say?"
Answer:	"They didn't follow the mountain - they went over what you call North Creek Pass. They camped on North Creek and then came over the Lake Valley Summit, and then took off to the right after they got into Spring Valley. Then they went in a kind of southeasterly direction where these cattle were running on the range, and they saw these cattle there, and they didn't see any shod horse tracks around there and thought it a good chance to get off

Modern Hereford bulls in an old juniper-post corral at the Swallow brothers' ranch. This corral was originally built for trapping wild horses. — Special Collections Department, University of Nevada Reno Library.

with a bunch. It was about dusk, or just before dark, and they took them on to a place what they called the "Troughs," over the line into Lincoln County, known as the Bailey Troughs."

Lew had made it sound so good to Bill, telling him it was a way to make some easy money. But they hadn't made a penny, and now Bill was in court, and Lew was hiding somewhere. The last time Bill had talked to Lew was that night when they loaded the stock on the train. Lew had gone with the cattle to sell them.

Question: "Where is this place they took the cattle from, as he stated to you. I mean what County?"

Answer: "It is in White Pine County."

Mr. Jurich: "Go ahead, now."

Answer: "He said they came in there and watered those cattle, then drove them in places and

kind of kept them hid up in the
daytime in the hills, and the like, and
drove them across the valley at night,
and got out of this part of the country,
and finally drove them by what is known
as Antelope Springs, in Utah - Then they
loaded them at night in Oasis."

Question: "At where?"

Answer: "Oasis, Utah."

Mr. Jurich: "Go ahead."

Answer: "Then, they were shipped from there and
billed to Denver."

Question: "To Denver, Colorado?"

Answer: "Yes, sir."

Question: "What else did he say? Tell us all
that he said."

Answer: "He said he was figuring on meeting him
(Hackbury) at Colexico, in Mexico
or Arizona, or in California. They
were going to get horses there -
catch horses there and ship them, and
he said afterward he overheard a
conversation in a barber shop there."

Question: "In what place?"

Answer: "In Oasis. They (the townspeople)
suspicioned something was wrong with
these cattle. They didn't think they
(James and Hackbury) were the bona-fide
owners. He (James) got his horses
then - he already had a ticket before
that time to Provo, Utah. He goes
to work then and gets his horses
and goes out - I just don't recall
the direction - I believe Mr. James

claimed to McIntyre's ranch."

Question: "North of Oasis, wasn't it?"

Answer: "Yes, sir."

Question: "You say he stated to you he had already bought a ticket to Provo, Utah, and overheard this conversation in the barbershop, and for that reason he didn't follow the cattle?"

Answer: "Yes, sir."

Question: "How many horses did he say they had, if you remember?"

Answer: "I think they had two horses."

Question: "You didn't give him signed authority or any right to take these cattle - to him or to Hackbury, did you?"

Answer: "No, sir, none whatever."

Question: "Do you remember anything else that he stated to you, Mr. Swallow?"

Answer: "Well, of course, preceding that he stated he had been working for Mr. James Reardon, down here."

Question: "In connection with these cattle, I mean - did he say when they loaded them?"

Answer: "I asked him when they loaded them and he said he wasn't positive of the date at the time. The record shows the date."

Question: "What time of day or night, did he say?"

Answer: "I believe he said they loaded them at night — after dark — ten or eleven o'clock."

Question: "Did he say anything as to where the cattle

were kept until they were driven into town?"

Answer: "Yes, he said they were kept out about ten miles from Oasis. He held them out there while Mr. Hackbury went in and engaged the car for the cattle."

—Courtesy Special Collections Department, University of Nevada Reno Library.

Bill paid little attention to the trial after that; he brooded over his horses. He missed that mouse-colored grulla and his gray pack horse.

The trial progressed, and Mr. Lockhart established the fact that Lew Hackbury was the principal offender in the crime and that Bill was an accomplice. The state then rested its case.

On April 17, 1915, Bill appeared in the district court and changed his plea from not guilty to guilty. The easygoing cowboy, who had gone along with all these adventures for fun, was convicted of grand larceny by Judge McFadden and sentenced to twelve to fifteen months in the Nevada State Prison at Carson City, Nevada.

The Nevada State Prison at Carson City, Nevada. (circa 1915) — Nevada Historical Society, Reno.

In a consuming state of depression, Bill was hardly aware of the good cattle country he was being escorted through on his way to prison. As he stared at the handcuffs on his wrists he thought of his last run for freedom.

After dodging out of that barbershop in Oasis, Bill circled toward some mountains, hoping to leave his troubles behind him.

> After I got out of the town lanes I hit out for a range of mountains where I could find water and plenty of grass for my horses. I rode the whole afternoon and all that night to get to them mountains, and I'd got above the foothills of them, where I found a little sheltered meadow with a small stream running by it. The grass was white with frost and there was snow amongst the granite boulders. It all looked like a mighty fine spot for me to stretch out my bed and take on a lot of something I hadn't caught up with for many a day, sleep. I took my bed off the gray horse, spread it out, picketed the gray and turned Smoky loose, and then crawled into that bed.
>
> *Lone Cowboy, My Life Story*, Will James.
> Copyright © 1930 Charles Scribner's Sons;
> copyright renewed 1961 Auguste Dufault.
> Reprinted with the permission of Charles Scribner's Sons.

Two sheriff's deputies riding from Fillmore, Utah, hoping to head off the fugitive, stopped at the well-known meadow to water their horses. They were downright lucky, for there was their wanted man sleeping like a baby. Bill was rudely awakened.

> Something was pulling against my shoulder, like a willow that bent but wouldn't break. I was dreaming that I was chasing some wild pony and got caught in a limb. When that limb kept a holding and pulling on me, I stirred up, and I found myself blinking into what looked like the mouth of a volcano. It was the busiest end of a forty-five six-shooter.
>
> "To bad I didn't have a little bit of sleep and could think a bit, I says to 'em. I'd been up above the spring then and watched you fellers go by."
>
> *Lone Cowboy, My Life Story*, Will James.
> Copyright © 1930 Charles Scribner's Sons;
> copyright renewed 1961 Auguste Dufault.
> Reprinted with the permission of Charles Scribner's Sons.

A herd of mustangs was rimming around a rocky butte in plain view of the sheriff's car, and Bill looked right at them as they drove by, but Bill was preoccupied and didn't see them.

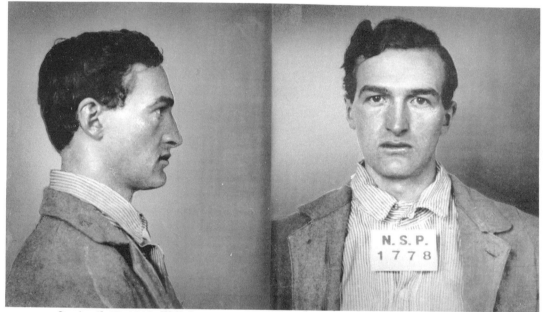

On April 17, 1915, Will James was convicted of grand larceny for cattle rustling, and he was sentenced to twelve to fifteen months in the Nevada State Prison. — Special Collections Department, University of Nevada Reno Library.

In *Lone Cowboy* Bill wrote that he had thought about the "hole card" he'd had in his boot, a .38 revolver, and how easy it would have been to "get the drop" on the two officers. The thought of this had scared Bill. He wrote that he had slipped the gun out of his boot and chucked it out of the car window and into the sagebrush alongside the road.

Bill was locked in a cell at the prison. The walls seemed to close in, and confinement was extremely hard for him. "That place could hold a mountain lion," he wrote. Bill was despondent; he longed to be free, roaming the deserts of the country he loved. "Now I know what a mustang feels like when corralled," he told one of his infrequent visitors at the prison.

48

Day after day and night after night he thought of the mountains and the deserts. He remembered the good feelings he had when there was a saddle horse under him as he rode along, free and independent. The following incident remained vivid in his mind, and years later he wrote about it in a story called "Midnight" that appeared in his 1931 book, *Sun Up*.

He thought of a little log cabin set in a grove of quaking aspen trees. It was a typical cow camp with a sod roof and a round breaking corral nearby. Several other corrals snugged up against the round one, with a horse pasture along the creek.

Bill remembered telling his mustang-running pardners that he was getting "chicken-hearted" and just couldn't take freedom away from any more mustangs. The men divided the wild ones into equal shares, and Bill did some horse trading to deal his pards out of a nice, black stallion. Bill's horses were roped, and a front leg of each horse was tied to its tail to prevent the herd from traveling too fast. The horses were lined out across country, and when they came to the cow camp, all were hazed into the corral. Bill then told his compadres to head back to camp as the mustangs were now herd-broke well enough to handle by himself.

He didn't sleep well that night, Bill recalled; he had a nightmare about the fate of some mustangs he had caught. When he awoke he found it hard to believe he was getting sentimental about those horses. He remembered walking down to the corral and looking in.

"The black stud is closest to me and kinda protecting the mares and younger stock," he wrote in *Sun Up*, "there's a look in his eye that kinda reminds me of a man waiting for a sentence from the judge. . ."

Watching the black horse reminded Bill of the way he had felt one time when stranded in a large city. Bill had been so homesick for the desert and mountains he would have given his silver-mounted spurs to be back in the range country, if only for a day or so.

Bill knew he was going to throw money away, but he just couldn't help himself. He caught all those horses and took the ropes off their front legs. The last one was the black stud, and Bill hesitated

Sun Up by Will James,
published in 1931.

because he did like the looks of that horse. "Then my rope sings out once more," he wrote, "in no time his front foot is loose, the gate is open, and nothing in front of him but the high ridges of the country he knowed so well."

As Bill lay on his prison bunk he envisioned the mustangs making their getaway. The bunch had floated along hardly touching the ground and slowly melted into the distance as free as the breeze.

Bill's world was made up of the clanging of steel doors, as he and the other prisoners were locked in their cells at night. Bells rang to tell them when to eat and when to sleep. Always there were crowds of men and the confining walls.

Bill received one consolation: the view outside his cell window where he could look at sagebrush hills in the distance and see stock grazing. He had no interest in any of the hobbies offered him nor in any of the duties he was assigned to. "All I knowed was riding, and that outfit sure didn't care for me to do any riding, so I was put to one job after another."

Bill had little in common with anyone until he met a cowboy who had gone on a wild spree and received a stiff sentence for his

50

behavior. This bowlegged "feller" reminded him of an old friend of his, a cowboy by the name of Lloyd Garrison.

At night as Bill lay in his cell, his mind drifted to more exciting times, like 1914 in Medicine Hat, Alberta, when he and Lloyd and another cowboy named Ronald Mason were riding broncs in a small rodeo.

Ronald Mason, who was better known around rodeos years ago as Crying Mason, was a good bronc rider, but he was also a bellyacher. He always was wanting a re-ride. In recalling those days, Mason said that when he knew Will James, Bill was as good a bronc rider as he had ever seen, and that was quite a compliment from a chronic Crying Mason.

As Bill went through the daily routine of prison life, he spent more time thinking over incidents from his past. He thought of the experiences that had made him the man he had become. He had painful memories of some of the first jobs he took on as a teenager while learning to be a cowboy and he felt that he had paid his dues.

He started out on roundup as a lowly camp flunky. Bill soon found when setting up a roundup camp that speed was all important. The flunky dug a shallow pit and started a fire immediately so that it

Tools of a range kitchen. Left to right: axe, coffee pot, cutter for making "bear sign" (doughnuts), meat cleaver, wooden spoons, spatulas, long forks with wooden handles, knife, steel for sharpening, hash knives, "gotcha' hook" for lifting hot dutch ovens, dutch ovens, shovel, and pot hook in foreground.
— Photo by Eva Bramlett.

51

burned down to cooking coals. He brought out the many dutch ovens and then drove two steel rods with an eye in the top of each into the ground on each end of the pit. He ran another steel rod through the eyes and hung pot hooks, shaped like an 'S,' on the rod. When food was cooked in the deep, cast-iron dutch ovens they were hung on the pot hooks to keep the food warm.

The cook pinched off sourdough to form biscuits, which he placed in the dutch oven. The three-legged oven was then set into a mixture of live coals and ashes. Red hot coals were shoveled on the dished-in lid. The biscuits cooked evenly to a golden brown.

Other flunky jobs included chopping wood and helping to stretch the tent that connected to the chuck wagon, providing shade from the sun and shelter from the rain and snow. Bill remembered peeling potatoes and washing dishes.

Bill didn't last long in the range kitchen. When he was offered the job of nighthawk he jumped at the chance. But he soon tired of that job too because he spent all night watching after the remuda, and when he was sleeping during the day the cook awakened him and told him to drive the wood wagon each time they changed camp. Most wagons on roundup moved once or twice a day.

Bill was proud of his next step upward in his climb to be a cowboy in those early days. The job of wrangatang (day wrangler) suited him fine. He herded the remuda. The remuda is to Montana what the cavvy is to the Northwest, the supply of saddle horses maintained by a cattle ranch. It was the job of the boy or man to see that the horses were kept together and at hand when wanted for work. A wrangler's social standing in a cow camp was close to the bottom, for his job was considered the most menial form of cow work, and he was the butt of all jokes from the professional cowhands. His job was a training school, and many good cowboys got their start wrangling horses.

After moving to a new campsite he penned the horses in a temporary rope corral to be ready for the cowboys when they changed horses, which was usually three times a day. The men worked the herd several hundred yards away from camp and the youth would

Montana's LV Bar roundup crew at noon meal. The "remuda" is penned in a rope corral where the horses and the wrangler will wait for the riders to rope their mounts.
L.A. Huffman photo, (circa 1914) — Montana Historical Society, Helena.

sometimes sneak over to watch. During these times Bill was never popular with the roundup cooks because any job that couldn't be accomplished from the back of a horse was a job he avoided. He went on to become a top hand as a bronc rider and cowboy.

Bill was a good athlete. As he drifted around the northern cow country he picked up knowlege on each ranch that helped him do a better job on the next one. He soon learned it was a good idea to ride through the small outfits and go to work for the big ones, so there was no danger of having to get off his horse to fix a fence or do other manual chores. The big ranches had men the riders called "rosin-jaws," who could not speak English, to do the ground work; a cowboy only worked cows from the back of a horse.

The days were long and monotonous at the prison and Bill just existed for awhile, days running into weeks and weeks running into months. He knew that in the game of life, just as in a game of poker, you ante when your turn comes and play the cards dealt to you, and for now, prison was the hand he'd been dealt. Bill wanted to stay out of trouble, and had no thoughts of trying to get away. He simply wanted to do his time and walk out a free man who "wouldn't ever be jumping whenever a dry limb cracked."

The making and handling of rawhide reatas *is an art. Of Spanish origin,* reatas *can vary in length from 50 to 80 feet.* — Photo by Eva Bramlett.

At the prison Bill met a Mexican craftsman whose work he admired. The penniless Bill cussed his luck, for the Mexican had recently finished braiding a fine, weighted bosal that Bill wanted for breaking horses. The craftsman offered to sell it cheap. "No *mas dinero*," Bill said sadly, meaning no more money. The Mexican grinned at Bill's attempt to speak Spanish and then handed a rawhide reata to him.

The reata was perfectly balanced with a button braided into the honda to give it weight when it was thrown. The loop would shoot out for an amazing distance. Bill was so lonesome for anything cowboy that he would have enjoyed taking the stack of rawhide coils to his cell to use for a pillow.

That night as Bill lay awake on his bunk his thoughts drifted to a *"rancho el grande"* in old Mexico where he had worked. He later told Gene Smith, a young cowboy he rode with in Arizona, how those dark-skinned Mexican cowboys could handle a reata. Their rawhide ropes varied in length from sixty to eighty feet long. Many times he had seen one of those vaqueros make a ten-foot loop and cast it all the way across the corral. The honda would zip down the rope as it sailed along, and the loop was the right size to fit over the head of the cow or calf when it arrived. In that sunny land of *"manana"* it was considered bad manners to get in a hurry and drag a calf by its head to the branding fire, for that was considered cheating someone else out of a job. Everything was roped by the head and then double-hocked, from the smallest calf to the largest bull. Many times he had seen a dark wisp of smoke coming from their dallies (the turns of the rope around the horn) on the large wooden pommels as they allowed the rope to slip and run with the animal.

> About the only thing they done which I admired was the way they handled their ropes. They sure had me beat in throwing any kind of rope, but I made many a vaquero jealous wih my riding, and the meanest of their horses was just pets to me. I was used to the big Northern horse, and any Southerner that's rode them would say that there's a heap of difference.

As Bill thought back he remembered how he hadn't liked the personalities of some of those Mexican horses in his string. They were nervous and distrusted people. However, after he left Mexico and drifted into Arizona he rode some horses and mules he had trusted with his life.

Arizona had been tough country. It had cactus-covered lowlands, rocky mountainsides covered with brush, wild cattle, and stickers on everything that grew up out of the ground. There were some real hands in that country, leather-covered men who rode with their lariats stacked on the saddle horn so brush couldn't tear the rope off as they raced through the chaparral after wild cattle.

Those Arizona brush-poppers were the fastest ropers Bill had ever seen. A cowboy would race after a wild thousand-pound steer with no thought for personal safety. No brush patch was too thick or country too steep for their tough horses; they stayed in hot pursuit. Those horses had been born and raised in that rough country and had legs and hooves as hard as steel.

When a cowboy spotted an opening in the brush ahead, he would push within roping distance, grab the "twine" off the saddle horn, and throw a little bitty loop out there with the speed of a bullet. "They could catch anything that walked or flew," Bill wrote.

Many ropers built a loop, figure-eighted it, folded the loop in half and hung it on top of the coils. When the cowboy needed the rope in a hurry, his loop was already built. All he had to do was to shake it out.

Rusty Criner "sitting on a hold-up," where a bunch of cattle are held in the open and the wild "cactus-boomers" can be driven to them from the surrounding hills. Rusty was a top hand on Arizona cattle ranches. Note the "hog-nosed" tapaderos covering his stirrups and two-piece branding iron alongside a dehorning saw tied to back of saddle.
— Bramlett photo.

Bill thought of the excitement when a full-grown outlaw steer was caught. It was tripped by throwing the belly of the rope around its tail end, and when the cowboy rode off to the side the steer's head was jerked the other way, and the rope swept its legs out from under it. The steer was tied down and six to ten inches of its sharp horns were sawed off. The sharp edge of the tipped horn was rounded by using a rock to hammer the edges down, or the edge was trimmed with a knife. Then it was tied to a tree overnight. The next day when its head was good and sore it was led out. A top Arizona cowboy could sometimes lead in two or three steers at the same time if all went right and he was lucky.

Bill began to get the hang of things, and enjoyed capturing wild cattle. He hired on at T.C. Wilder's Yolo Ranch sixty miles northwest of Prescott, where he teamed up with a young cowboy named Gene Smith. Bill traded Gene out of an old pair of hog-nosed tapaderos because that stickery brush was wearing his boots out.

The pride of each of those southwestern rock-hoppers was in bragging on how many "orhannas" he had caught. The term "orhanna" comes from the Spanish word *orejano*, which means long-eared, and incudes all slick-eared, unbranded stock. When an "orhanna" was spotted it was roped as soon as possible, tied down, earmarked, branded, and castrated if needed.

Gene was a top roper, and he kidded Bill about his big "motherhubbard" loop that caught in a lot of brush. Bill had ridden open country most of his life and threw a big loop a long way. In order to keep up with these wild desert cattle, "cactus-boomers", he went to a smaller loop and rode closer to throw it.

As he lay there in the darkness of his cell, Bill had to laugh when he thought about the circumstances that led to his getting fired from that ranch.

Bill and Gene had been in that wild cow camp for two months or more, and they had run out of supplies. They caught up their horses and a couple of pack mules, then headed up country toward the ranch headquarters. They had ridden 35 miles and were within a mile of their destination when a shoe on Bill's horse started clinking. He dismounted to pound on the shoe with a rock to tighten it. While the two mules were cropping grass, Gene rode on ahead to check out three head of stock he'd noticed.

Gene came racing back all excited. "ORHANNAS!" he yelled at Bill, "Let's capture 'em!" Bill hastily mounted his horse and then, as Gene Smith said, they "punched holes in their ropes and spurred ahead."

The three yearling bulls didn't even get excited as the riders approached them. They had the appearance of being stamped from

Although getting "long in the tooth," Gene Smith was still all cowboy, pictured here in the 1960s. He had been foreman of Prescott, Arizona's Yolo Ranch for 20 years.
— Bramlett photo.

Always well-mounted, Gene Smith shod his own string of horses. (circa 1960s) — Bramlett photo.

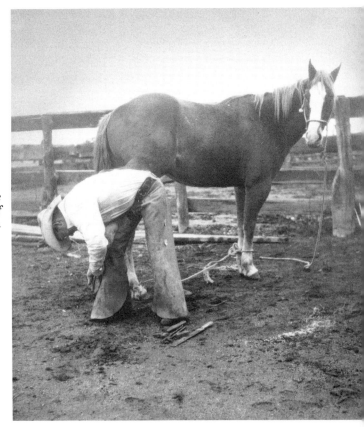

58

the same mold, with deep red bodies, white faces, and horns curving downward. In no time at all those bulls were roped, tied down, castrated and branded with the short, two-pieced running irons all Arizona cowboys carried with them. The men completed the job by unsheathing the little dehorning saw from Gene's saddle and proudly tipping the horns on the newly-made steers. Now, all who saw them would know they had been caught and marked.

The two cowboys were in a state of excitement when they arrived at headquarters. They were surprised to find the ranch had acquired a new foreman while they were in camp. When the cowboss introduced them to their new boss they wasted no time in bragging to him how they had branded and castrated those three "orhannas." Purple-faced with rage, the new foreman fired them both on the spot. Bewildered, the two young men cornered the cowboss and asked a few heated questions of him. The cowboss couldn't help laughing a little as he told them those three orhannas they'd castrated were actually expensive Hereford bulls the new foreman had turned loose on the range to upgrade the stock. They were not branded because the Eastern-raised foreman figured the tatoo in their ears would be enough to show ownership.

Eventually Bill quit resenting prison so much, and doing time was easier for him. He made trusty and was put in charge of feeding and exercising some horses the guards stabled inside the prison walls for chasing escaped convicts. ". . .even tho I mixed with horses during the day," he wrote in *Lone Cowboy*, and pranced 'em around a

Arizona cowboy Monk Maxwell (Gene Smith's nephew), keeping his "eyes peeled" for "orhannas." Note the heavy leather, shotgun chaps with "tie-down" ropes hanging from belt. (circa 1966) — Bramlett photo.

59

bit, I was craving often to be free on one, and wanting wide open country, some place where I could do as I pleased."

When the guards discoverd Bill's ability as an artist he was furnished with plenty of paper and pencils, and Bill repaid the guards with drawings. His drawing board was the lid of a grain box.

This phase of imprisonment became one of Bill's turning points. His thoughts continuously dwelled on the wide, open country he had roamed for years and the horses he had ridden. He now had time to do concentrated drawings from his limitless memory; his drawing techniques improved rapidly.

Bill was informed of an opportunity to appeal for parole, and he wasted no time in writing the prosecuting attorney and the justice judge before whom he had appeared in the Ely, Nevada, courtroom. He wrote the following letter in his own careful handwriting.

The Board of
Pardons & Parole
Carson City Nev

State Prison
Aug 19 – 1915

Gentlemen
 I herewith submit for your consideration an application for my release and parole.
 I was sentenced april 28 - 1915 from Ely to from 12 to 15 months on a plea of guilty to Grand Larceny I was in jail 7 months and have thus served altogether 11½ months.
 I am a young man 23 years of age and this is the first trouble of any nature I was ever in

I have a natural talent for drawing and during my imprisonement have done considerable of this work, It is my ambition to go East and study Art and I feel that if given an opportunity to develop this talent my future will be assured, As a sample of my work I am submitting for your inspection, a few samples drawn by my-self.

During my imprisonement I have had ample time for serious thought and while this experience is unfortunate and to be deeply regretted it has not by any means embittered or discouraged me and if given an opportunity I feel I can go out of here and live and upright and honorable life and be of some use not only to myself but to my fellow man

I assure you Gentlemen that if my plea is given favorable action I will endeavor to live in such a way that you will never have cause to regret your kindness

Respectfully Submitted
Will R. James
Nevada State Prison

— Special Collections Department, University of Nevada Reno Library.

By Will James. — Special Collections Department,
University of Nevada Reno Library.

Bill sent this letter along with his well-known drawing that shows the past, present, and future of his life. The past shows him roping a steer, the present shows him doing time in prison, and the future shows him painting.

Bill also sent along a letter he had received from Justice Judge H.W. Edwards which read in part:

Dear Will:

Glad to hear that you are going to make an effort to obtain a parole and sincerely hope that you succeed. I do believe that you have rid your system of this foolish idea of going back to your old employment, riding at forty dollars per, why say, a school kid can earn that much money, and a full grown man such as you are should be worth considerable more.

When you get out make up your mind to go ahead with your drawing and make something of yourself. Governor Dickerson is a mighty fine man and if he finds out that you are in earnest, I am sure that he will do what he can for you.

All the boys here, as you know, are quite friendly toward you and they feel as I do that you let someone else talk you into stepping off the Straight and Narrow path. And nothing would please both the boys and myself to hear that you are successful in your endeavors to get a parole and then try and make something of yourself.

With Best wishes and trusting that you will get your parole, I am,

Sincerely yours,

Judge Edwards

Bill's hopes were high when he attached the following letter from the prosecuting attorney, Anthony Jurich, to the others.

August 10th, 1915.

Mr. Will R. James,
Carson City, Nevada

Dear Sir:

This will acknowledge receipt of your letter wherein you informed me that you will ask for a parole.

In this respect I may add that in my opinion, if your conduct has been satisfactory there, the Board of Pardons should grant you parole.

I do not feel that you are beyond redemption, in fact from what I know of your case I am satisfied that you did not fully appreciate and realize as to what you were doing when you committed the offense for which you are serving time.

I feel that Hackberry who was associated with you in the matter and who we have been trying to locate for some time is by far more to blame than you are, in fact he was the leader in the transaction.

Respectfully yours

A. Jurich

The letters and drawings were obviously not enough, for Bill's parole was denied. He became extremely depressed. It would be a long six months before he was allowed to apply again.

By March 15th, Bill had a new letter typed and ready to submit. Although his time was mostly served, he could not wait any longer than necessary to get out. Years later he told Alice he had felt like a caged animal and could not tolerate further confinement; he longed desperately for freedom.

"To my way of thinking anybody with a lot of nerve can't be all bad."

— *Will James Book of Cowboy Stories*, Will James.
Copyright © 1951 Charles Scribner's Sons;
copyright renewed 1961 Auguste Dufault
Reprinted with the permission of
Charles Scribner's Sons.

Bill certainly had a lot of nerve and he produced a bogus letter offering him employment, signed by a star of the silent movies, William S. Hart. Ironically, Bill was to meet the actor in later years. He also submitted the following letter:

Nevada State Prison
March, 15th, 1916

Honorable Board of Pardons,
Carson City Nevada.

Gentlemen:

I Respectfully request that I be granted a parole at the coming meeting of The Honorable Board of Pardons in April.

I was sentenced April 28th, 1915, to from 12 to 15 months from White Pine County upon a plea of guilty to a charge of Grand Larceny, And when your Honorable body meets April 10th, I will have served nearly one year and will have little more than one month yet to serve.

I was denied a parole by your Honorable Body last September,

64

but was given permission at that time to apply again in April 1916.

I base my plea for clemency upon the fact that my time expires May 18th, the next. And I have performed all the work Assigned me faithfully and to the best of my ability.

I have employment awaiting me in California and it is my intention to go there immediately upon my release and earnestly endeavor to live as every man should live, respectfully, upright and honest.

I am enclosing a letter from William S. Hart, offering me a position, and request that same be returned to me after the coming meeting of the board.

Will R. James,

Respectfully Submitted

— Special Collections Department,
University of Nevada Reno Library

When Bill's parole was finally granted he was handed a sack containing the clothes he'd worn upon arrival at the prison. They were unclean and badly wrinkled, but when he shoved his hand to the bottom of the sack and felt the spurs on the heels of his boots, everything was just fine.

The warden handed Bill ten dollars in "gate money" and the front gate was opened. On April 11, 1916, good times started again for Bill when he strolled out of that prison a free man.

The walk into town felt good to the bow-legged cowboy. He spent the night in a cheap hotel, ate some restaurant food, and began his search for a job. A bartender told Bill a man named Bill Dressler of the Plymouth Land and Livestock Co. was in town looking for hired help.

Bill found Mr. Dressler and asked him for a job. When he discovered the job was "pumping cows" he didn't bat an eye, but talked as if he'd milked cows all his life. Bill mailed a request to the parole board for his papers and then departed for the farm in Smith Valley,

Nevada, with another hired hand. Early the following morning he took on those black and white Holsteins.

At no other time in his life would Bill have considered milking cows for a living. He had always been disdainful of working at any job where he wasn't a-horseback. This job was acceptable because it removed him from the vicinity of the prison. Bill had become physically soft during his incarceration. His arms ached and his hands swelled in two weeks of trying to milk cows. He ignored the pain though, because he felt so good to be living in that beautiful valley.

One evening as the sun dropped behind the peaks of the Pinenut range, Bill stood leaning against the barn as he rolled and smoked one Bull Durham cigarette after another. He studied the wonderful changes of the light in the sky.

Transfixed, he turned to face the desert mountains on the eastern side of the valley. He noticed that as the sun lighted the tops of the peaks a misty, blue color began at their base and slowly rose until the hills appeared to be floating. Suddenly a horse and rider emerged from that blue color.

Curley Fletcher, born in 1892, the same year as Will James. Their trails crossed 24 years later at the Rickey Cattle Company, and they both went on to achieve immortality through their written work. —

66

A cowboy rode toward him on a snorting, glass-eyed horse. When the young rider maneuvered the side-stepping pinto around for conversation, he asked Bill about some stray range stock. "Ain't seen any stock except these damn Holsteins," Bill answered. "By the way, I'm Bill James."

"Glad to meetcha, Bill," the cowboy replied. "Folks call me Curley Fletcher."

"Say, Curley," Bill asked, "does your outfit need any more hands?"

"Matter of fact, we do," Curley replied. "Can you ride broncs?"

"I can ride anything that wears hair," Bill said with conviction.

"You'll work out fine then, but what are you doing on this farm?"

"Trying to pump some milk from these cows," Bill muttered, "but I sure as hell ain't gettin' much!"

When Bill explained his situation, Curley laughed and said he'd be back *manana* with another horse and saddle. When Bill turned in his time and drew his wages he had a feeling this was a case of quitting before he was fired.

The curly-haired cowboy arrived the following day at noon, leading a saddled horse. Bill hadn't been on a horse for a long time, and it felt good and natural as he settled into the saddle.

"You must have borrowed this rigging from a feller my size," he told Curley. The pair left the farm and rode along a lane as they headed toward the southwest corner of the valley. In that corner the Pinenut range sloped down to form a gap where the Walker River

Nevada's Wellington Mercantile as it stands today in Smith Valley. — Bramlett photo.

cut through. In the distance above the gap Bill could see blue and white peaks simmering in the summer sky.

Curley had some cattle penned in a holding pasture behind the Wellington Mercantile. They dismounted and lounged on the wide, shady porch of the country store and drank sodas.

"Well, let's get to it," Curley finally told Bill, and the two horsemen rode to a fenced pasture behind the schoolhouse. Curley rode into the pasture and roped a scrawny, gray horse. He led the horse over to a tree where his rolled-up bed lay under the branches. Bill held the gray's head down by its ears to distract it while Curley lashed his bedroll to its back. The cowboys then bunched the cattle and started them traveling along trails following the river.

Bill James felt good to be on a horse driving cattle again. His heart sang a song with the bubbling river as he looked at the gray, yellow, and rust-colored peaks that rose on both sides of the canyon. A few miles along the river, the terrain changed and the country opened up. A few more miles beyond, as they pushed the herd over a sandy point of land, Bill suddenly saw the prettiest sight he had seen in over a year. Huge, blue mountains with snow-covered peaks made up the Sierras on his right, and the colorful ranges of the Sweetwater Mountains spread out to the left.

"There's Topaz country," Curley drawled as he nodded toward the green valley in between the two ranges.

The Walker River west of Smith Valley, Nevada. — Bramlett photo.

68

The bronze plaque reads in part
TOPAZ POST OFFICE
Near this location records show
establishment of a post office at
Topaz, Mono County, California,
February 20, 1885. Nearby were a
school, way station, blacksmith
shop, and other facilities of the
Rickey Land and Cattle Company
operations.
Bramlett photo

The cowboys lined the cattle out to higher ground to avoid some boggy areas. Green grass was "knee deep to a tall bull" in the pasture where the riders left the cattle and then loped off toward a stand of cottonwoods in the center of the valley. Cattle dotted the landscape as far as the eye could see.

As Bill rode by buildings of the Rickey Land and Livestock Company, he immediately liked the place. On his left was a long stucco building that had wide swinging doors at each end. This was the blacksmith shop. Forty yards west was a schoolhouse, started as a one-room building but now with a room built on each end. Across the road to the north a post office stood in a clearing alongside the Way Station, which also served as a store.

The two horsemen turned onto a trail that wound through a grove of cottonwoods to a small cabin surrounded by corrals. They unsaddled their horses and carried their rigging into a room at the end of a long barn where looped ropes hung from the rafters. Here the cowboys hung their saddles, out of the reach of pack rats that might chew the sheepskin off the skirts to make nests. Curley stuck one of these loops down through the gullet of his saddle, then looped it up and over the horn. Bill did the same.

The pair strolled over to the cabin. As Bill walked in behind Curley he noticed the similarity of this camp to others where he had lived, worked, and played. A wooden table and chairs dominated the center of the room. A deck of well-worn cards, a coal oil lamp, and a sardine can ash tray sat on the spur-scarred table top. A wood-

69

The Rickey cow camp
it stands today. Will
James rode the outlc
roan in the round cor
in foreground. He
bunked in the cabin.
— Bramlett photo.

burning cookstove with its stovepipe stuck in a brick flu and two wooden bunks nailed to each corner completed the furnishings. Coat hooks were mounted on the wall above the bunks, and below was a magazine clipping of a thoroughbred stallion of racing fame. A door by the stove led into a smaller back room where bedsprings lay on the floor with a rolled-up bedroll on top.

Curley threw his bedroll on one of the bunks and then introduced Bill to Dave Reed, a cowboy with one leg in a cast. The shy cowboy immediately built a fire in the stove and began peeling potatoes.

"Leg feel any better?" Curley asked him.

"Aw, a little I guess," Dave said. He grinned and then added, "That damn roan!"

The following morning Curley sent word to headquarters that he had found someone to assume Dave's job as bronc buster. The three men ambled over to look at Bill's new string of broncs. There were ten head in the horse pasture, none of which had been handled except for two that Dave had started. In a corral by himself was a strawberry roan that Bill instantly figured for an outlaw. Bill grinned because he knew things were going to get interesting.

The roan has a more or less uniform mixture of sorrel (reddish brown) and white hairs over its body, with more white on its rump.

A strawberry roan. — Bramlett photo.

The head, mane, and tail are a sorrel color, as are the stockings that come up to its knees and hocks.

"How come that ol' roan is penned by his lonesome?" Bill asked Curley. "Is he a stud?"

"About halfways," Curley replied.

"Oh, an ol' "original"," Bill said with a laugh.

Seeing the roan in a separate pen was no surprise to Bill. "Originals" tend to fight other horses. An "original" is what a cowboy calls a horse that is a little studdish. When it was castrated as a colt, only one testical was cut off, the other remaining inside and never dropping, giving the animal the temperament of a stallion rather than that of a gelding.

The "snorty" roan horse was wearing a 44 brand on its left hip, showing it had belonged to E.G. Harlow, a rancher from Fallon, Nevada. It had a sullen look in its eyes that haunted Bill all day.

That evening Bill forgot the roan as he inspected his borrowed saddle. It was truly a dandy piece of equipment. The saddle had been built the previous year by the famous Mexican saddlemaker G.S. Garcia from Elko, Nevada. When Bill discovered the saddle be-

71

1915 G.S. Garcia saddle, today a collectors' item. Many dignitaries, such as Will Rogers and Douglas Fairbanks, rode Garcia's saddles, and buckaroos thought nothing of shelling out a full season's pay to own one. — Photo by Eva Bramlett.

longed to young Dave and that Dave was anxious to head home to be with his folks while his leg healed, he immediately began dealing with him for the well-built "hunk of rigging." He paid Dave all the money he had and promised to send the balance as soon as he was paid. He also bought Dave's hackamore set-up. The bosal on the hackamore was strong, braided rawhide with a rawhide core and a heavy heel knot. The headgear had a sliding leather blind attached to it, with a cotton fiador and a three-quarter-inch horsehair McCarty that looped around for reins. It also had a long lead rope that could be tucked under a rider's belt. Bill was now ready to begin breaking horses.

A story told with relish by Bim Koenig (1911-1986), of Coleville, California, took place the day Bill went to work on that string of broncs.

A crowd had gathered, and when Bill put the hackamore on the horse's head, he pretended to put it on backwards. The crowd had a good laugh, but after the lanky cowboy rode that bronc those laughs turned to cheers because Bill could ride bucking stock better than any cowboy they had seen.

Each morning began the same for Bill. He would throw the roan some hay and run the other broncs into a large corral in front of the cabin. After closing the gate he crowded the bunch into a round

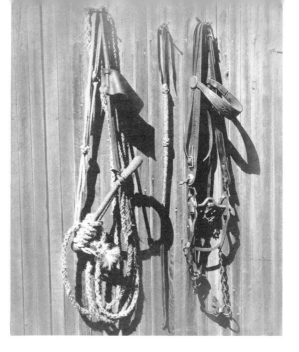

Vintage cowboy equipment. Left to right, hackamore set-up for breaking horses, rawhide quirt, and early 1900s-style bridle with buckle on top for ear-soured horses.
— Photo by Eva Bramlett.

corral attached to the larger one. He would then rope the horses to be worked that day and turn the others loose.

As the weeks passed, Bill enjoyed life to its fullest. He felt good to be a-horseback, and he had a nice string of broncs developing into riding horses. There was always an audience cheering him on when he bucked out those broncs. He felt he really could ride anything that wore hair.

One day on "rodear" Curley asked a dreaded question. Bill was holding a small bunch of cattle in a corner of the corral while Curley did the sorting. As Curley cut a snaky pair out of the bunch and shoved them past Bill, he yelled, "Are you gonna ride that damn roan, or will I hafta ride him for you? The roundup crew will be back soon, and I'm gonna leave to join my wife down at Bishop."

Bill knew he had been putting off riding that horse for a long time. When he looked at the Roman-nosed outlaw he wondered if he could live up to his brags and really ride him.

That evening, as the cowboys arrived at camp, they noticed strange horses in the pasture and smoke coming out of the chimney. Upon entering they were happy to see the Rickey Company foreman sitting at the table with an old friend of Bill's, a cowboy named Fred Conradt. The two had ridden down from Bridgeport country that day.

73

Welcome visitors to the cow camp, Fred Conradt and friend. — Special Collections Department, University of Nevada Reno Library.

The men ate beef, beans, and 'taters, and later the talk turned to the weather, cows, feed, and horses. The foreman mentioned the roan a few times. As Bill sat on the edge of his bunk rolling another of his ever-present cigarettes, he knew the time had come to saddle the outlaw.

The following morning Bill ran the roan into the round corral. He was glad big Fred Conradt was there to help him because when his loop sailed over the roan's ugly head, Bill had his hands full. This was the hardest fighting horse he had ever encountered. There was no give to the animal. Bill took his turns around the heavy cottonwood snubbing post in the center of the corral, and the roan finally choked down some and fought to a standstill.

Fred leaped up and wrapped his arms around the horse's neck and got an ear between his teeth. He chewed for all he was worth while Bill tied some hobbles on the roan's front feet. Next, they wrestled the horse around until they got the hackamore on its head and the blind pulled over its eyes. The horse stood there blowing and trembling as Bill threw his saddle on its back and cinched it tight. He tucked the lead rope of the McCarty under his chaps belt, pulled his hat down snug, loosened the hobbles, and stepped on.

Fred cleared out of the round corral and watched through the gate as Bill leaned over and raised the blind. The roan blinked a couple of times, his head dropped out of sight, and he let out a roaring "beller" as he exploded underneath the cowboy.

When the horse was sunfishing he made the highest dive of any horse Bill had straddled. The punishing jolts were coming so fast and hard Bill couldn't keep up with them. He was getting dizzy and his nose began to bleed. He hoped to stay in the saddle a little longer and build a reputation to be proud of, but it wasn't to be.

Bill soon lost his hat, and when he felt the right stirrup go he lost his balance. He faintly remembered that high dive as he hung in the air briefly before crashing to earth. Fred and Curley were there when Bill hit the ground and dragged the limp cowboy through the gate to get him away from the roan.

The roan had barely warmed to the fight. He bucked and fought and fell down several times. He stepped on the McCarty rope hard enough to loosen the headgear and finally shucked it off. He bucked and "bellered" until he loosened the saddle and the blanket slipped out and fell to the ground. Then the saddle turned and rolled completely under the horse's belly. The roan kicked the saddle with his hind feet as he bucked around the corral.

Bill liked his Garcia saddle, and he wasn't planning on standing there while a "jug-headed outlaw" kicked it to pieces. He grabbed a lariat and ran to the center of the corral, followed by Fred. The two of them threw several loops at the horse, and Bill finally caught the roan by the front legs and it went down. Fred ran over and sat on the horse's neck and twisted its head back while Bill hustled over to tie the horse's legs together. As Bill bent over the horse from the top and tried to snare a hind leg with the tie rope, the roan kicked forward at the saddle that was still on its belly, and a powerful hind leg caught Bill in the jaw. The cowboy was layed out cold.

When Bill regained consciousness he had a pounding toothache. His teeth hadn't been in very good condition, and the kick had loosened and split most of them. The pain was increasing rapidly. His friends told him he had no choice but to go to a good dentist and get those "choppers" fixed.

A couple of days later Fred saddled up his horse and lashed his bedroll to his pack horse. He rode over to Bill, who was stretched out in the shade of a giant cottonwood tree.

"I'm headin' on down to Reno," he told Bill. "Why don't you ride along with me? You can get your teeth fixed there and stay at my folks' house, no charge."

Fred laughed at the sight of Bill sitting there with a rag tied around his head and his jaw discolored and swollen. "You ain't a very purty sight right now," he said, "but I've got a bunch of sisters and they're all full of hell." Bill declined the offer, and Fred rode north.

Curley was next to bid Bill "adios." He told Bill that he and his wife and brothers were heading back to Arizona to put on some rodeos.

"I'll never forget that fight you had with the roan," he told Bill.

Curley Fletcher was the same age as Bill, and his life had been equally as colorful. The day after his wedding in 1914, he and his wife Minnie departed for Cheyenne, Wyoming, to ride in the rodeo. Curley won money bronc riding and Minnie earned a few dollars trick riding, but Curley became involved in a crap game and gambled away their combined earnings. Curley's mother had to send them tickets to come to Arizona.

Curley Fletcher and wife, home from the wedding. Next stop, Cheyenne. (circa 1914) —
Courtesy

76

Curley shootin' craps with the boys. —

The Fletcher brothers put on bronc-riding exhibitions throughout the Gila Valley and passed the hat among the audience. Monetary rewards were not satisfactory, so Curley wrote his famous poem *The Outlaw Broncho*, which was printed and sold to their audiences. The poem described a roan-colored bronc.

One year after Will James' ride on the roan horse, Curley polished up his bucking horse yarn and renamed it *The Strawberry Roan*. An unknown German balladeer put the lyrics to music. The song was an overnight success and will live forever as one of the favorite cowboy songs of all time.

Before his departure the well-traveled Curley advised Bill to go to the big city of Los Angeles to find a good dentist. Bill was concerned about his "bridle teeth and grinders" and wanted them fixed correctly. Fall was approaching and the nights were getting cold. The cooler the nights, the more his jaw ached.

Bill turned in his time and bought a bronc from the ranch. Then he rode to the nearest railroad and followed it until he came to some houses and a water tank. "I sold my horse there," he later wrote in *Lone Cowboy*, "sacked my saddle and took it along with me as I hopped on the first train that stopped."

Bill enjoyed his first train ride. Watching the country roll by and daydreaming a little as he listened to the steady clickety-clack made him drowsy. He woke up as the train pulled into the downtown Los Angeles depot. To his surprise, it was the morning of a brand-new day.

77

His number one priority being to find a good dentist, Bill threw the sacked saddle over his shoulder and headed out the door. A taxicab driver stopped him and offered to help, so Bill hopped into the cab and was driven across town to a dentist the cabbie knew of.

This dentist examined Bill's mouth and informed the cowboy that the dental work required would take two months to complete. He gave Bill a price and made a string of appointments. Bill tossed his saddle over his shoulder again and strolled out into the street looking for a cheap hotel. He found one in the next block.

Those first weeks were lonesome ones for Bill. He was homesick for the range country. He longed for the company of a horse or even the company of a man who smelled like a horse. He couldn't afford to spend money because he didn't have enough green stuff to pay the dentist and maintain himself as it was. He walked around a lot, up and down the beach and around that end of town.

Bill located a saddle shop and hung around there for awhile looking at saddles and rubbing the engraving on the silver-mounted bits. The clerks began watching the lean cowboy as he handled the expensive mouthpieces, so Bill made a hasty exit.

The four walls in his room would close in on him as soon as he walked in the door, and he would head out to walk the streets again. He went to the dentist every other day, and in between visits he simply existed.

It's always darkest before dawn, and so it was with Bill. He was moping around, thinking he couldn't handle the city much longer, when he heard hooves pounding on pavement. He looked up and there was the "purtiest" sight he had seen in many days. Four sure-enough cowboys were riding along through the streets. He followed them for several blocks, and then he really "seen a sight for sore eyes." The riders left the pavement and rode into a real Western town.

Bill must have thought he'd died and gone to heaven because that town looked as if it had been moved from the range country of Nevada or Montana and plunked down in the middle of the city. Instead of stone and brick buildings with automobiles in the streets,

Cowponies.
— Photo by Eva Bramlett

here was a real cow town.

There were corrals full of horses, pens of longhorn cattle, buckboards, stage coaches, and even some Indians walking along with feathered war bonnets and war paint. Bill doubled back on his tracks; he didn't want to forget where this place was.

He spotted the four horses the cowboys had been riding tied outside a saloon. Bill sauntered up to the swinging doors and looked in. He began to feel right at home when he overheard an argument between a dally man and tie-hard man. One of these "fellers" looked and sounded familiar to Bill. It suddenly dawned on him that here was a cowboy he had worked with in the past.

"What the hell do you know about a double-rig and a tied rope, Sam?"

Sam whirled around, and when he saw his old friend standing there, his face split open wide with a toothy grin. He grabbed Bill's hand in his big paw and introduced the cowboy all around. Bill discovered this place was called Edendale, where the fledgling movie industry came to get cowboys, horses, and livestock for their Western pictures. There was a motion picture studio close by, and Hollywood was only a short ride away on horseback. Sam talked to Bill about hanging around and getting into the picture game. This sounded just fine to Bill. Sam kidded him by saying that Bill, with his face, could get a part if they ever needed a horse thief character.

The cowboys didn't have long to wait before going to work. The Thomas Ince Studio was beginning production on a silent Western movie called "Six Guns and Ropes" that would take at least a month to film. Bill was hired as an extra. Now he could make money while getting his teeth fixed.

One day the director called Bill over and stood him alongside the leading man. They were about the same height, and both had protruding chins; Bill became his double. The leading man spent much of his time with the leading lady, and when a dangerous horseback stunt was planned they ran Bill in to take his place.

"We was made to ride thru many bad places that day," Bill wrote in *Lone Cowboy*. "By the time that day's work was done I got to wondering if I had any of the fillings left which the dentist had put in my teeth."

Bill wound up with a sprained ankle as a result of bucking a horse over a bank and down a twenty-foot drop. He had to lie around a few days to mend, rubbing horse liniment on the ankle to ease the pain. He complained to Sam how he did all the dangerous stuff and the leading man got the credit for these stunts. Sam laughed and told him that was the difference between a man who worked with his head and a man who worked with his hands. Bill threw a boot at him.

In a big chase scene, Bill rode with a posse, and Sam was with a band of desperados. The posse cornered the outlaws, and the part Sam was playing called for him to break loose and make a run to escape. Bill was dressed in the leading man's clothes and was directed to give chase to Sam. The fun-loving boy in Bill took over, and he couldn't seem to stop himself from doing what came next. He took the lariat rope off his saddle, and when Sam broke loose he fired a big loop out there, catching Sam around the middle. Sam's eyes bulged, and he was very surprised when he hit the ground, for there was Bill sticking a six-shooter in his face, telling him he was the one that was a sure-enough horse thief kind of character.

Bill fully expected to be fired for his moment of weakness, but he wasn't. The scene was shot over again, and the work continued. The posse corraled the outlaws. The leading lady was rescued once again and went riding off into the sunset with the leading man. Years later Bill wrote about his brief acting career in a short story entitled, *Filling In The Cracks*, from the book, *Sun Up*, 1931.

Five weeks of steady work was finished for Bill when the movie was completed. The director called him over and said he liked the sequence where Bill had roped Sam and hoped to use it in the film.

Bill went in for his final appointment. His dentist appreciated the business Bill was giving him but was surprised to see Bill getting all that work done on his teeth because most young men his age were waiting to let the Army do their dental work for them. Bill made a mental note to check in with his draft board the next time he passed through that part of Nevada.

The rainy season began, and all filming stopped for awhile. The cowboys hung around the Jones stable, which they considered their headquarters. They were waiting for calls from the studio. As he loafed, Bill enjoyed watching the Hollywood girls go by. He later described them as ranging from "running to draft stock."

Jones welcomed the cowboys to put up at his place, but he expected them to keep busy repairing equipment and do the breaking and training of horses.

"That James kid," Clarence Jones recalled in 1966, "was the laziest of the bunch, unless he was on top of a horse. One reason I remember him, and hundreds of cowboys have floated through here in the past fifty years, was because of his drawings. For a

Anthony Amaral, 1930-1982, author of the book, Will James, The Gilt Edged Cowboy. — Courtesy Nellie Laird.

81

while they were tacked all over the place. I only have one now, dated 1916. After James left here, his pictures began to disappear from the barns and sleeping quarters, so I grabbed the one I considered the best."

—Anthony Amaral
Will James the Gilt Edged Cowboy,
Westernlore Press, 1967

The fog and steady drizzle continued for weeks. When the weather finally gave the movie people a break, a call came in to the Jones stable wanting a hundred riders and all the horses, cattle, wagons, and oxen Jones could put together. A promise of six weeks steady work was made. Everybody was excited and raring to go, except Bill.

With the coming of spring Bill was homesick for the desert cattle ranges. He could close his eyes and picture little white-faced calves sunning themselves in spots where the snow had melted away and green grass was sprouting. Nevada buckaroos would be running in the cavvys soon and preparing to go on roundup.

Bill just couldn't tolerate town any longer. He told the director he was quitting, and he drew his time. When he told Sam *adios*, Sam wasn't surprised, for he had seen a faraway look in Bill's eyes right after the grass turned green.

"Doggone it, Bill, I hate to see you go," Sam told him. "'Cause you're the only one I like to argue with around here. Besides, I need to git even with you for that little roping trick of yours."

The two friends shook hands, and Bill sacked up his saddle in a gunny bag and headed for the depot. He bought a ticket to Tonapah, Nevada, on the next train north.

. . .

The dust boiled twenty feet overhead as the cattle were driven down country. Five hundred pairs of cows and calves and an odd assortment of other cattle made up the herd. It was the result of a two-day gather on the Pine Creek Ranch in a section of the Monitor forest. The herd was held in big corrals at the end of a rugged but spacious valley.

Nevada buckaroos branding calves. (circa 1916) — Courtesy The Northeastern Nevada Museum, Elko.

Beef stew, biscuits, and a boggy-top pie were hot and waiting for the men in the big Dutch ovens at camp. After the noon meal, the cowboys went to rope their herd horses. Bill caught a well-broke horse out of his string, knowing today was his turn to rope and drag calves.

Most of the steers, bulls, and dry cows were cut from the herd, along with some stock a "rep" from a neighboring ranch was waiting to trail home. There were six ropers and two branding crews. When the irons were hot, the ropers were given a nod and the branding began. Bill hadn't roped a calf in a long time, but he was eager to get at it. Roping calves was fun; it was Christmas and New Year's all rolled into one for most buckaroos, and Bill was no exception.

He eased his horse into the herd of cows and immediately spotted a calf within range. He flipped his rope under the calf's belly and tried to make the loop wrap around its hind legs. When the calf jumped ahead Bill only had one leg caught so he shook the loop off. On all of the outfits he'd worked for in Nevada, a roper didn't drag any calf unless it was caught by both hind legs. When he threw the next loop the honda hit the calf's hock and stopped as the belly of the loop wrapped around its hind legs. Bill dragged the calf over to the branding fire, and he and his horse held it by the hind legs as the crew branded and earmarked it. When the calf was castrated, the testicles were tossed into a bucket for a "mountain oyster" fry.

When all the smaller calves had been worked over, the large

Nevada buckaroos castrating a horse. (circa 1916) — Courtesy The Northeastern Nevada Museum, Elko.

calves were roped by the head and dragged out to the open ground between the herd and the fire. Here they were heeled and then stretched out for branding. Some of the full-grown stock was roped and doctored, and a colt that was running with the cavvy was fore-footed and heeled, after which it was castrated. The works finished, the crew rode back to camp.

Bill had received word from that "feller" in Utah that his horses had either been stolen or had drifted back to Nevada. He began to feel restless.

"As much as I like my job," he wrote in *Lone Cowboy*, "a same old failing of mine began to get a holt on me again. That was to drift."

Bill decided to draw his wages and ride north, keeping "his eyes peeled" for any sign of his smoke-colored horse.

Bill meandered through the mountains and deserts of Nevada over remote stock trails until he arrived in Elko, a busy cowtown in northeastern Nevada. He made his usual visit to the Garcia Saddle and Bit Company on Railroad Street.

While eye-feasting around the place, he met the cowboss of the old Spanish Ranch from up around Tuscarora and was hired on to help with the roundup.

This part of the country, with its huge sprawling ranches and hardly any fences or branding corrals, became a big favorite with Bill. Cattle were worked in the style of old-time, open-range outfits.

G.S. Garcia, the famous bit, spur, and saddle maker who was a favorite of all old-time buckaroos and has become an important part of our Western tradition and heritage.

Today the business is known as Capriollas. — Photos Courtesy The Northeastern Nevada Museum, Elko.

Most of the buckaroos in this country were real horsemen and had several handy spade-bit horses in their strings of saddle animals. These were finished bridle horses that could throw themselves after a cow with style.

Spanish Ranch buckaroos.
(circa 1917) — Courtesy The Northeastern Nevada Museum, Elko.

85

Suppertime for the roundup crew on the Spanish Ranch.
(circa 1917) — Courtesy The Northeastern Nevada Museum, Elko.

Bill enjoyed living at the wagon that summer, but he heard rumors about a war going on and that the government was calling in men who had registered. All the riders were talking about it, and some had already enlisted. Bill sent a letter to his draft board, but before he received a reply the roundup was over, and he had sold his horses and boarded a train to Malta, Montana, where he went to work for the Circle Dot outfit.

The following year, Bill discovered he was in serious trouble with the draft board. The letters they had sent to him had arrived after his departure to a new range. When the word finally caught up with him, he was on the verge of being labeled a draft-dodger. Bill immediately quit his job and started across country to check in with his draft board. He knew he would soon be in the Army.

In August, 1917, Bill stopped over in Calgary, Canada, and went on a drinking party with some of his friends, Bob Standley, Sleepy Epperson, and Calgary Red. The partners then joined another buddy of theirs, Lloyd Garrison. When Lloyd told them he was in the Canadian Army and was home on a month leave, Bill sobered up fast and bade them all farewell. He said he was crossing the border to join the Army.

The remaining cowboys decided they would go on the road, make a few rodeos, and ride some broncs. They all loaded up in Red's

86

Model T Ford. The first show they went to was at Taber, Alberta, where they ran into Bill. Bill grinned and said the Army would have to wait a little longer as he jumped into the Ford, and they all headed for the Taber Rodeo grounds.

Bill planned to go on one last party before becoming a soldier boy. To start things off right, he drew bucking horses and cowboys all over the Model T with colored crayons. They had admirers in every town.

The fun-loving cowboys went on to make the shows at Moose Jaw, Saskatchewan, The Big Gap out of Hardesty, Alberta, and then down to Medicine Hat, Alberta.

Riding high at the Moose Jaw Rodeo.
(circa 1917) — Special Collections Department, University of Nevada Reno Library.

Their last night in Medicine Hat the cowboys put on a show in the street. Bill had acquired the nickname "Bullshit Bill" on this trip, so naturally he was the announcer. Calgary Red did some rope-spinning tricks, and Sleepy Epperson played the harmonica. All the boys sang a few songs, but they attracted a nice crowd anyway.

They decided the next thing they should do was ride a bucking bronc down Main Street. The sheriff happened to be in the crowd, and he put a halt to that line of thinking.

"Come on, boys," Bill told them, "I'm treating you drunken skunks to a picture show."

When the boys had arrived in town Bill couldn't help but notice the name of the picture that was playing at the local movie house. It was "Six Guns and Ropes."

Calgary Red argued that a picture show was a little tame for rip-snorters like themselves, but Bill insisted. They entered the theater and sat down in the front row. The movie started with a bang, and the men made comments on what a good rider that leading man was. Bill didn't mention it was he doing those daredevil stunts because they wouldn't have believed him. He was waiting for the scene where he roped Sam off his horse. He was anxious to hear one of his pards say, "By Gawd, there's Bill!" But the movie ended, and to his dismay Bill realized that the roping scene had wound up on the cutting room floor. Disappointed, he bade his friends another farewell and headed down country toward Nevada.

In early May, Bill strolled into the draft board in Winnemucca, Nevada. On May 20, 1918, he was inducted, assigned to headquarters company, 21st infantry, and sent to Fort Kearny, California.

Bill had to put aside his lightweight, handmade boots and wear heavy brogans. His comfortable, old sombrero was exchanged for a stiff campaign hat and his shirt, vest, and levis were replaced with an olive drab uniform and canvas putees.

His early days at the army cantonment were spent getting inoculations and drilling. Bill did spend his share of time on K.P. He laughingly said he was afraid for awhile he would have to help win the war by peeling potatoes.

Bill's toes didn't turn out as many a walking man's feet do. They turned in, for he was a rider who had worn spurs all his life. He was only afoot during the first month and a half of his Army time. Soon he had migrated to that side of the cantonment where the horses and mules were stabled and trained.

Working with horses was for enlisted men only, but when Bill showed the officers how well he could ride, a major who needed more

Will James had to exchange his cowboy "duds" for an olive drab uniform and canvas putees. (circa 1918) — Courtesy Clint and Donna Conradt,

cowboy help pulled some strings. Once again Bill was a-horseback.

He sent for his saddle and riding gear and went to work bucking out and gentling the horses the Army was buying. The specifications the buyers used had to do with how a horse was built and not how well he was broke. Some of those *caballos* were well-built outlaws right out of the Western range country.

Bill was later transferred to another company as a mounted scout. He found this wasn't a popular job because when they crossed "the big pond" he would be the first person to get shot at. Bill didn't worry as long as he was a-horseback. The way he had it figured, he could at least die with his boots on.

Bill was in the Army over nine months, and he never was shot at.

89

Working with horses was for enlisted men only, but Will James soon talked his way to the other side of the army cantonment where the animals were stabled. (circa 1918) —

The war suddenly came to an end and the armistice was signed. Unfortunately, he couldn't leave for home right away like most of the other soldiers because he had to stay to help dispose of all those horses and mules.

The days dragged by until he was released. That same night he boarded a train, and with his saddle in a gunny bag, Bill headed back to cow country. He planned to get some horses and wander around for a while to see if he could find that old smoke-colored horse of his.

Bill was wide awake the next morning when the sun peeked over the mountains in the east. Golden sunlight flooded the white sage plains, and to him it was a "mighty purty" sight as he looked out the window of the train at all those miles of lonesome. He felt a little

Will James and friend on leave. (circa 1918) —

90

fluttery feeling inside when he spotted a golden eagle diving toward some hidden prey in the sage. As the miles clicked by he began to see scattered bunches of cattle and a few wild horses off in the distance, and Bill's heart felt good.

He thought back and reviewed many of the events that had taken place in his life. Like most people, he'd had his ups and downs. He was human, but he had met life head-on with no backing down.

"One thing's for sure," he mumbled out loud, "I can say I was a-horseback wherever I went — in prison, in the movie pictures, and even in the Army."

In the latter part of Bill's life, a group of singing cowboys recorded many songs about range cowboys. They were called The Sons of the Pioneers. One of their songs, written in 1934, must have been inspired by the lifestyle of Will James, the drifting cowboy.

Tumbling Tumbleweeds

Sung by Bob Nolan and the Sons of the Pioneers

See them tumbling down
Pledging their love to the ground
Lonely but free I'll be found
Drifting along with the tumbling tumbleweeds.

Cares of the past are behind
Nowhere to go but I'll find
Just where the trail will wind
Drifting along with the tumbling tumbleweeds.

I know when the night has gone
That a new world's born at dawn
I'll keep rolling along
Deep in my heart is a song
Here on the range I belong
Drifting along with the tumbling tumbleweeds.

— RCA Victor Recording Co.,
"Cool Water" album, 1959

HERES HOPING NO SNOWDRIFT EVER STOPS YOU OR SETS YOU AFOOT-
AND THAT, AS FAR AS ALL GOES, IT'S SPRING TO YOU ALL THE TIME

Will James sits on his horse and Elmer Freel holds the team as Fred Conradt snaps a picture of their wagon with a string of broncs tied on the rear. — Courtesy of Clint and Donna Conradt, all rights reserved.

Chapter III

HAPPY AND THE ONE-ELEVENS (III's)

Reno was my turning point. I rode my last good bucking horse there and went to slinging paint instead of swinging a rope. It was in 1919, when getting tired of the deserts I'd been riding in I thought of drifting north into Oregon where timber and water wasn't so scarce. I stopped over for a few days in Reno and learned that a rodeo was going to be pulled off. I went to see the manager to learn all about it and wound up by selling him a few drawings to advertise the rodeo with. That was the first work I'd ever sold and it sure tickled me to see that I got the same as two months wages for that two day's work.

Will James, *Nevada State Journal,*
October 26, 1924

IN MARCH OF 1919 a lone horseman stared intently at a mountain to the west. He watched as two eagles circled in the updrafts of an escarpment of rock. A triangle-shaped opening of a cave showed

Fred Conradt, 1892-1949, broke broncs for California's Long Valley Ranch in 1919. —

in the rock and one of the birds set its wings and darted inside.

Fred Conradt's eyes traveled aimlessly toward an adjoining peak, and he noticed with mild interest that the huge knob of the mountain resembled the shape of an elephant's head. Below the peaks and to the south, smoke billowed from a sawmill at the town of Loyalton, California. As Fred's eyes took in the scope of country and the little town, he thought of Dolly Trosi, his sweetheart who lived there, and he wondered what she was doing on this day.

Fred suddenly realized he would be running out of daylight if he delayed longer, and he wheeled his horse and rode over the pine-clad ridges that separated Sierra Valley from Long Valley. As he trotted along he searched the ground for tracks of a certain bunch of range horses.

The lone rider was working his way down a rocky, sage-covered ridge when he located fresh horse tracks. Fred rimmed around the adjoining points, hoping to jump the horses before darkness overtook him.

A loud piercing snort from the shadows of a stand of pine trees brought his search to an end. He spurred ahead to the trees. An old mare shot out of the cover followed by several other mares with little colts. Two geldings brought up the rear. As Fred raced downhill behind the herd he looked over the geldings. They were five-year-olds, the correct age to start on work they had been bred and raised to do.

When the herd arrived at the creek traversing Long Valley, Fred swung wide to turn them upstream. He raced along the top of a high cutbank where he could keep the bunch in sight as they plowed up the sandy creek bottom. Several miles upstream was a trap, and he hazed the horses into this large corral. He then cut the geldings into a smaller corral and turned the mares and colts back onto the range.

Early the next morning the cowboy tied a saddle horse to a fence outside the corral and strolled into the enclosure with a long catch rope. He sized up the two five-year-olds. They were like most cow ponies of the early 1900s. Bred of mustang-cross mares and studs that carried the strains of thoroughbred, Steeldust, or Morgan bloodlines, these colts had some size to them. The bald-faced sorrel had flat bones and the long musculature of a thoroughbred cross. He weighed about eleven hundred pounds, maybe a little less. The black colt that ran at his heels looked a good twelve hundred pounds. The black was short-legged and long-bodied with heavy muscles on its hips and legs.

The two colts raced around the corral. They rolled their eyes and tossed their heads, always keeping an eye on that human critter. The long-striding sorrel was out front when he felt a rope circling his front legs, jerking them out from under him. When first roped by the neck, some horses will throw themselves over backwards with such force they can break their own necks.

Before the sorrel was aware of what happened, those same legs were tied up to his hind ones, and the bowlegged cowboy was sitting on the colt's neck fitting a hackamore to its head. A fiador was then

Fred and his new wife returned to Long Valley Ranch, where Fred accepted a job as foreman.

cinched up on its jaw to hold everything in place. When freed, the little horse leaped to its feet with plans of hightailing it away from there, but Fred hung on to the other end of the soft, cotton rope that was tied to the hackamore.

The horse fought for its head and plunged into the rope, but the human took a wrap around a post in the center of the corral. Like a fly fisherman playing a trout, the leather-covered cowboy played the fighting horse. He held the rope tight to stop the charge but gave it slack before the colt went over. Finally, when the little horse was worn down, the cowboy mounted his saddle horse and worked the sorrel through a gate in the corral. Closing the gate, Fred eased the bald-faced five-year-old to some tall grass patches along the river and tied the other end of the rope to a log that was lying there for that purpose. He then rode back into the corral and went through the same procedure with the black colt.

After two days of being staked out to logs, both the sorrel and the black colt were a little skinned up and sore, but they'd learned how to give to the rope and were anxious to be led along.

Fred led the sorrel into a round corral and hobbled its front legs with gunny sack hobbles. Holding the soft cotton rope with his left hand, he sacked out the colt with an old saddle blanket. He started by fanning the air around the colt and wound up flopping it over the horse's back and around its legs. At first the colt wanted to climb the corral bars, and he fought the blanket, but gradually he stood there trembling and let the cowboy use the blanket to rub him down. A half hour of this and the cowboy dragged a saddle over to the colt. That spooky thing really made the little horse wild-eyed. In due time the cowboy was able to get his saddle on the sorrel, which ran off when the cinch was pulled tight. But the cowboy took a hip-lock on the rope and when the sorrel colt swapped ends, it'd had enough. The horse had new respect for a rope.

"Cheeking a bronc." After the first two or three saddlings most colts can be mounted by holding the horse's head to one side by the cheek of the headstall. Arizona cowboy, Mike Mcfarland, mounting Applejack. (circa 1969) — Bramlett photo.

The cowboy blindfolded the colt, untied the hobbles, and stepped on. When he raised the blind, the rodeo was on. The horse was scared and did a good, honest job of bucking. Its natural instinct was to get rid of that cowboy and the hunk of leather on its back, but the rider stuck like a postage stamp. Fred was good at what he did for a living.

The next day the colt was beginning to taper off on his bucking, and the man rode him outside. This cowboy was careful to keep the horse's spirit intact, and that's why he gave the gelding its head, allowing him to buck naturally.

Days passed and the sorrel resented the rider less each time he

97

was ridden. He continued to buck some at every saddling, but he became more interested in what the rider wanted him to do. When the cowboy started working cows on him, the colt enjoyed this job and forgot about bucking at all, except maybe on cold mornings.

To a bowlegged man there's nothing in this world like bringing a willing colt along until he becomes a good cowhorse. Cowboys enjoy looking at a pretty horse, but when there are cows to be worked, they are only interested in what a horse can do. A cowboy will ride hundreds of horses in his lifetime. Most likely, he'll only remember one or two as good performers. When you see an old pony that really tries to please its rider, you know that horse was handled correctly when it was being trained. The cowboy on its back was able to help that horse think each move was the horse's own idea. In other words, he asked the horse first, and only if that failed would he make the animal ante up.

The black colt was different. He would strike at the blanket and the saddle and with those quick hind feet try to pick the buttons off the cowboy's shirt. With ears laid back and fire burning in his black eyes, that colt made Fred stand back and take notice. The first saddling was twice as rough as the sorrel colt's first one, and the second saddling was even rougher. The black colt had no intention of giving up. Apparently his natural inclinations didn't include being saddled and ridden. The more the colt bucked, the more it learned about bucking, and the tougher it got at the game. It would buck hard three or four times at every saddling, and Fred was beginning to wonder if he'd be able to stick with the horse next time. When working cows, if Fred speeded up that black *caballo* to turn a runaway cow, it would break in two and go to bucking again.

Fred began to realize the horse was an outlaw. It would never give up and would remain independent of the human and always fight and tear things up. The horse was built right for fighting. It was hard as a rock, wild as a deer, and sure enough bad. Fred liked horses a lot and had never mistreated a horse in his life, but the black had no use for him.

When the spring roundup was over and the broncos, with the

exception of the black, were going good under saddle, Fred drew his wages and left Long Valley Ranch. He caught his two private ponies and rode east. It was an easy day's ride home to Reno, Nevada, where he arrived in time for the big rodeo.

Another bronc rider was on the verge of heading toward Reno town, although not by his own design. His trail would cross both Fred Conradt's trail and the trail of the black colt. This crossing would prove to be the important turning point in this cowboy's life, a turning point that would unleash the sleeping genius of a man destined to be one of the greatest horse artists and storytellers of this century.

Way down in central Nevada this bronc rider was getting his fill of riding the rough ones. This dark, slim buckaroo was thinking on a regular basis about riding to the other side of the mountains. It was Will James, and he was "baching" at a desert camp where he was "snapping broncs." He had been by himself for so long he would occasionally find himself talking to a joshua tree by his camp. It was a twisted, trange-looking cactus that looked to him like a tormented soul from hell.

The more Bill thought about it, the better he liked the idea of heading out for a country like Oregon that had some real trees and

In a Nevada cow camp, on a desert studded with Joshua trees, Bill has rare but welcome help as he stamps a calf with a hot iron. — Courtesy Clint and Donna Conradt, all rights reserved.

99

maybe hire onto some outfit working cows instead of bronc riding. Bill had reached a crossroads in his life, and he was thinking about quitting the rough ones. He'd had his share of broken bones from mounting numerous bucking horses.

Of riding bucking horses he once said, "It's a true born art, like it has to be with the painter or singer in order to be good at it." Bill often talked of the twisting, sunfishing, and side-stepping tactics of a good bucking bronc, and said no rider could stick for long unless he could feel these movements coming.

All those "snuffy ol' ponies" had taken a lot out of Bill, who began to dread getting on a new one. As he mounted up he could feel his legs shaking a little, causing his spur rowels to ring. To him that was a bell that tolled the end had come; it was time to back off riding the wild ones.

Bill drew his wages, saddled up his private horse, and tied his bedroll on a pack horse. Leaving the wall in the camp plastered with drawings of bucking horses, he rode north. He pulled up at the mining boomtown of Tonapah and in typical cowboy fashion went to the largest place in town to load up on ham 'n' eggs, at the Mizpah, a five-story hotel.

The Mizpah was a grand site, the pride of the town. The tallest building in Nevada for over fifty years, it was a Victorian testimonial to instant wealth. Bill cleaned his plate, and as he looked around he resented the elegance of the dining room with marble on the walls, velvet-covered chairs, and beautiful brass chandeliers. He resented it because it meant progress — more people, more houses, and more machinery on his beloved desert.

Bill wasted no time in saddling up and lining out his horses in a northerly direction. Riding off a long, sloping hill onto a large flat, he chuckled out loud at a herd of wild burros wringing their tails and braying as they rapidly moved out of his way.

Pulling up his horse, he looked off to the right at the rising blue ridges and thought of familiar trails heading to Montana country. He glanced left at the towering line of the Sierra Mountains with

*The cover of the 1919 souvenir
Reno rodeo program
featuring one of the drawings
Will James sold to rodeo
manager, Glen D. Hurst.*

their white fingers of snow reaching to the sky, fingers that seemed to beckon him to come.

As Bill sat there on his good little cow horse in that sun-drenched country he pulled out the makin's and dribbled a little stream of Bull Durham into a straw-colored cigarette paper. He rolled it tight and licked the edge of the paper so it glued shut. Twirling the end and putting it in his mouth, he lit up. Bill looked again at the mountains off to the right, and, with a sigh, reined his horse left. A few days later he stopped over in Reno and never made it to Oregon.

> The last bucking horse I rode is, or was a couple of years ago, about as good a bucking horse as there was in the West. I could just as well say in the whole world, because there's no fighting ponies nowheres that can come up with the western range horse of the U.S. on bucking ability that way.
>
> Anyway, he was some bucking horse, and many a bronc rider would tell you so. We called him "Happy" because he looked anything else but that. His head was about as long as my arm,

which is pretty fair length, and his body matched up with that head, but there the proportions ended, for his neck and legs was short and thick and didn't at all match with that head and body of his. I'd notice how, on account of his head being so long and his legs so short, he'd hardly have to bow his neck to reach for grass. He was built like one of these Dutch hounds, two horse long and one horse high.

But that build of him was all a feller could find to grin at about that horse, and the minute a feller got up in the middle of him, all grins, if there was any, faded away and a mighty concerned interest took place.

The One-Elevens (III's), Elmer Freel, Will James, and Fred Conradt. —

Happy was the horse that changed the course of Will James' life in that memorable year 1919. Ultimately, this black horse was to finish Bill as a bronc rider and start him thinking about a career in art and writing. It was the year Bill sold his first art work. The drawings were to be printed on rodeo posters and souvenir programs for two of the rodeos held in Reno, July, 1919, and 1920.

Bill had drifted into town earlier that year of 1919. Reno's first annual Nevada Round-Up Rodeo was going full blast, and he just naturally migrated in that direction. While he was hanging around this cowboy range carnival, he buddied up with two cowboys he'd rode with in the past, Fred Conradt and Elmer Freel. They became close friends, or as Bill put it, "The way the three of us kept together you'd think we was all handcuffed to one another."

They were a fun-loving trio, a trifle rowdy, and, unless they were a-horseback, just a little bit lazy. In typical cowboy style they identified themselves with a brand, the One-Elevens (III's); one stood for Bill, one for Fred, and one for Elmer. They made a pact among themselves that whoever of the three owned a ranch first would share it with the other two. To Bill this commitment was so strong that he even drew this trademark under his signature on many of his early works.

The One-Elevens broke a few horses, entered bronc riding contests, and Bill made fifty bucks illustrating those Reno Rodeo posters. As a general rule, however, they had one thing in common. All were flat broke. Spot cash was the missing element in their young lives. Town employment being out of the question for these three bowlegged knights of the range, they talked it over and came up with a simple solution: why not put on bronc-riding exhibitions and take up a collection afterwards? It was a case of no sooner said than done when Fred was able to produce three broncs, and he brought in three dandies. One was the black colt Happy.

Bill argued with the boys about which horse he would ride. He had always taken pride in his bronc-riding ability, but now he wanted to taper off a little. Fred chose the ol' rodeo tough, Hell-Morgan, a horse Bill shied away from because the outlaw had done such a good

In good spirits, Will James and Elmer Freel pretending to fight. — Courtesy Clint and Donna Conradt, all rights reserved.

Always at home on a horse, the One-Elevens were often seen "horsing" around.
— Courtesy Clint and Donna Conradt, all rights reserved.

The likable Elmer Freel, willing to do anything for a laugh. — Courtesy Clint and Donna Conradt, all rights reserved.

104

job of bucking in the Reno Rodeo two months earlier. Elmer took a horse named Soleray and Bill wound up with Happy, the ranch bronco they thought would be easy to ride.

They roped Happy out of the bunch and eared him down. As Bill slapped his saddle on the round, slick back, he had an uneasy feeling about using his new saddle. When he first came to town he had noticed his rigging was worn out, so he headed for the Bools & Butler saddle shop and traded his old Garcia in on a new saddle. This saddle was one of those newfangled roping rigs with a low fork and a little, low cantle. He jokingly said that all the cantle was good for was to keep a "feller" from sitting down. This proved to be very true.

Many cowboys like a flashy outfit, and Bill was no exception. He just couldn't resist a pair of twenty-six inch tapaderos to go over his stirrups and hang down. They were full flower-stamped to match the saddle, and the whole outfit was "mighty purty". Long tapaderos are great for sorting cows. With a little flick of the ankle you can wave them in a cow's face and turn the critter. However, they are no good on a bucking horse. Being heavy, they won't stay with your feet, especially when the taps are new and stiff. But, this being a practice session and all in fun, Bill just pushed his feelings of apprehension aside and cinched it down tight.

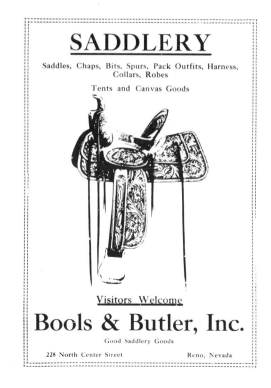

An ad from the 1919 Reno rodeo program that prompted Will James to trade in his old Garcia saddle on a new one.

They led the horse out to the open and blindfolded him. Elmer mounted up and stood by with his lariat rope ready to rope the black horse when Bill was through with it, or when the black was through with Bill, whichever came first. Happy spread out and stood spraddle-legged as Bill threw a leg over and settled into the seat of the saddle. He leaned ahead and pulled the blindfold off.

The horse stood for a brief instant, and then, to everyone's surprise, that twelve-hundred pound chunk of dynamite exploded into a series of hard, gut-twisting, pile-driving bucks. Happy didn't fire straight like most broncs. At the end of each buck he would hit the ground hard and spin backwards, then do something else and go right back to spinning. Those long tapaderos gave Bill a bunch of trouble. The horse kicked one off, the wind took the other, and that little cantle was punishing him each time Happy hit the ground. Those taps slapped Bill around as they swung like kites in a strong wind. Elmer spurred up alongside and between jumps asked Bill if he was wanted to "pick up" for him, but Bill just grinned and tried a little harder to get his feet inside the stirrups.

Bill was embarrassed in front of his pals for the way this ride was going. He wanted to show them he could ride with style, but the horse gradually slowed down to crow hops and Bill knew when it quit bucking that bronc would throw its head up and stampede out of the country.

Bill spotted a stand of trees ahead, and, not wanting to leave any hide hanging on those limbs, he pulled up his right leg, planning to swing it over the horse's neck and jump off. Suddenly he noticed railroad tracks underfoot, so he tried to slip back into the saddle, but too late. The horse had felt Bill move to one side, and he took advantage of that move. Happy spun to the side and came back sunfishing, leaving Bill hanging in thin air. He came down hard on the railroad tracks, cracking his head on one of the rails. As Happy sailed over him, Bill slipped into unconciousness.

After the wreck. "O bury me not on the lone prairie!"

A doctor was fetched on the run. During the half hour Bill was out, the doc pulled the torn scalp into place and bandaged his head. When Bill regained conciousness, Fred and Elmer helped him to his feet and steadied him on his rubbery, bowed legs. Bill felt bad about spoiling the fun for his two pards, and he attempted to keep things from becoming too serious. With a grin on his face he began to sing an old cowboy song, "Oh bury me not. . .on the lone prairie!"

A crowd had bunched up around him, and someone yelled, "He's out of his head!" Bill came right back at him, "You'd be out of your head too if you'd tried to bend a railroad track with it."

Bill was in the hospital for two days, where he received twenty-two stitches in his scalp. He recuperated at the home of Fred Con-

radt. Bill was twenty-eight when Happy convinced him he was too old to ride the rough ones. He was now ready to hang up his spurs and get serious about his art.

As for the bronc Happy, he went on to become a double tough bucking horse in a rodeo string, a horse that was seldom ridden to the whistle, and then only by a top rider. Hearing of the success of the outlaw, bucking horse, Will James wrote a story about him called *The Turning Point.*

> "I don't feel so bad that I put up such a bum ride, and was hindered with them long tapaderos, on the last bucking horse I straddled, because now I see where providence played a hand

108

Fred Conradt riding "the ol' rodeo tough," Hell Morgan, as a large crowd of spectators look on.

and someday I'd like to see 'Happy' again, and I'd like to touch his black hide in a sort of handshake from one artist to another — but sometimes, as I feel the scar that runs over the top of my head, I do wish I'd had my old saddle that day when I straddled 'Happy'."

All In The Day's Riding, Will James.
Copyright © 1933 Charles Scribner's Sons;
copyright renewed 1961 Auguste Dufaulte.
Reprinted with the permission of
Charles Scribner's Sons.

Elmer makes a good ride as Bill and Fred ride alongside to help. Small crowd of spectators to right of picture.

109

THE NEVADA ROUND-UP

THE Round-up as staged in Reno on the present occasion, the Rodeo of Salinas, Calif., and the "Frontier Days" and wild west celebrations of Cheyenne, Wyo., Pendleton, Ore., and Prescott, Ariz., are only another proof of the theory of evolution. To find the original, germ idea of this carnival-industrial event, we must go back to the days of the Spanish grants in early California.

California was the home of the stock raising industry in the West and had its own precedents and lore, handed down from the Indians to the dons and their descendents. From the golden state the cattle raising industry spread across the mountains into Nevada, Arizona, New Mexico and western Texas.

The pioneers of this movement carried with them the customs of the old Spanish-California rodeos, which were later transformed into the round-ups. As the trail moved northward through Colorado, Utah, Wyoming, Montana and the Dakotas, the lore of the rodeo moved, too, changed in a few particulars by environment, peculiarities of range and market and by other peculiarities.

Always, however, the strain of the old Spanish caballero and his rodeo fiestas has remained strikingly marked. In the early days the Hidalgos with a picked following of aqueros and their remudas of fine saddle horses would assemble at a certain hacienda or ranch and there gather the cattle from the neighboring hills for many miles, drive them to the rodeo grounds, brand, ear-mark and apportion them to the various owners and finally drive them to their respective holdings.

These rodeos lasted a week, sometimes two. During the day the serious and oftimes dangerous business of working the cattle engaged every able-bodied man present, while the evenings were devoted to amusement. With true hospitality the owner of the rodeo ground would kill and barbecue one or more calves or steers and everyone was welcome to partake of all he or she could of the delicious meat broiled over coals and washed down with copious draught of wine or stronger liquor. This meal continued more or less all through the night, but when the more pressing needs of appetite had been dulled, the soft tinkle of guitars and more penetrating notes of the violin heralded the commencement of the nightly dance, which usually lasted until the first silver streaks of dawn.

The men were picturesque in jackets and calzoners of leather or velvet, heavily trimmed with cords and buttons of silver, high heeled boots, silken shirts and costly sombreros, the women in silks and laces, eyes flashing or languishing behind the inevitable fan and the watchful chaperons observing every action.

At the dances of earlier days there was very little class distinction, the poor and rich associating on equal terms. When a woman was a skillful dancer she had a good opportunity to display her graces. The men would become enthusiastic and applaud her and as a mark of special appreciation would place their hats on her head, one on top of the other; and as her head could bear no more she would the hats in her hands, dancing all the Still more hats, and even coins were thrown her feet, and when she returned to her these were gathered up by the tecolero brought to her. All the hats in her posse had to be redeemed by owners with coin, each pa what he pleased from reales to five dollars.

When the ball broke u men accompanied the w to their homes playing m When the female element been disposed of the went into the street on h back and sang. Tired o they would practice las the stock and generally up the festivities with a tended bout with brandy.

Next day this pro would be repeated with ations, and the festi would be continued until women and beasts were nigh exhausted. After a days rest, the gayer o young vaqueros would away to some other and distant hacienda, where other rodeo or round-up to be held. The ranch ov vied with one another in viding entertainment for guests. Gambling en later into the rodeo sports and this in the resulted in many serious gun duels.

It is a far cry from pastoral times suc those to the sordidly practical twentieth tury, but young blood ever runs hot and modern cowboys and cowgirls emulate and pass their forbears in those old, stirring past risking life and limb for the applause o crowd and ascendancy over possible rivals.

The center-page spread of the 1919 Reno rodeo souvenir program.

The following write-up appeared in the 1919 Nevada Round-Up Souvenir Program:

THE COWBOY ARTIST

Introducing Will R. James, cowboy artist.

Noticed the posters for the Round-Up and Fourth of July celebration?

Better notice them right away if you haven't, for they are the work of a so-far-undiscovered genius of the range who may some day rank with Charlie Russell or Frederick Remington.

Like Russell, James is a real cowboy. He has ridden the range from Montana to the Mexican line and back for years. And all the time he has kept busy with his pencil or crayon. Without any technical training he learned to draw the life of the range and round-up as he saw it with accuracy and action that stamp genius all over his work.

How James remained undiscovered for so long is one of the mysteries with which real genius is wont to wrap herself. He "sifted" into town a few weeks ago, headed for the Topaz Ranch to get another job cowpunching. He heard of the Round-Up, located manager Glenn D. Hurst and asked him if the latter cared to see any horse pictures. "Bring 'em on," said Hurst. After glimpsing a few of the amazing pictures which James had drawn, Mr. Hurst "signed" him on the spot.

First Annual Nevada Round-Up
Souvenir Program, 1919

Alice Conradt 1904-1985. —

Chapter IV

MARRIAGE AND A NEW CAREER

*"I rode for most all the biggest cow and horse outfits through
the U.S., Canada and some in Mexico, and I think it funny
sometimes that with all the countries I've seen that I should pick
on Washoe Valley to settle down in. Maybe it's because here's
where I turned and left the trail of the range for the trail of art."*

Will James, *Nevada State Journal,*
October 26, 1924

IN 1916 ALICE CONRADT came riding down Virginia Street at
the head of a rodeo parade. She was mounted on a good-looking,
high-stepping horse and rode well.

The American flag in her hand billowed in a sudden gust of wind.
The breeze went on to stir her golden hair as her blue eyes sparkled
with excitement. If Will James had been standing among the crowds
that lined those streets, no doubt his heart would have "skipped
many a beat" at the sight of this pretty girl.

The parade meandered to the Rodeo grounds, and the contests
began. Alice Conradt gave the flag to an official and proceeded to
her prominent seat to watch as the first saddle bronc rider was
bucked off. Little did she know that on that very day the man who
was to be her husband was being bucked off a roan outlaw horse
eighty miles south of there in a Topaz, California, cow camp.

Old-time parade in downtown Reno, Nevada. — Nevada Historical Society, Reno.

Alice had five brothers and six sisters. Her youngest sister, Agnes, laughingly said that Alice received what the other girls didn't. Alice was tall and slim, and, as a buckaroo once described her, "It didn't hurt your eyes any at all to look at her!"

'Pappa' Edward Conradt was a superior wood craftsman, a builder, a contractor, and he had interest in a lumber yard and mill. Both parents were born in Germany but met and were married in Hawaii. Eventually they settled in Nevada, where they raised a

Ad from the 1919 Reno rodeo souvenir program.

Alice with mother and father Conradt on their way to the train station to bid Will James farewell on his trip to San Francisco. — Courtesy Clint and Donna Conradt, all rights reserved.

114

Like a dream come true, it was love at first sight for Will James and Alice Conradt.

houseful of kids. The family lived in a two-story, brick house on the Scanavino Ranch, way out at the end of West 5th Street.

In those days Reno was a big cow town. Growing up in its indolent outskirts was easy for Alice. She could ride all the way to Sparks, back to Moana Springs, and then home on a streetcar, for a nickel.

In 1919 Reno had its first annual Nevada Round-Up Rodeo and Alice's brother, Fred, came to town for the show. He brought a friend of his home for dinner, a buckaroo by the name of Elmer Freel. Elmer was a likeable, easy-going guy who was always clowning around and teasing Alice and her sisters.

Then one day Fred brought another friend home, and this time the fifteen-year-old Alice paid attention. She felt immediate interest in the dark-haired stranger. Bill noticed Alice too, and from then on, when someone opened a door, there stood a grinning Bill.

He gradually moved in with Fred. He seemed to be around at mealtimes and the laundry grew in size, but Alice's sisters didn't mind because they all liked the lanky cowboy. He helped them with their homework, drew pictures for them and told them stories about the wild country.

When Bill was thrown from the bronc and injured, only a quarter of a mile south of the Conradt house, one of the Conradts rushed for the doctor. After being in the hospital for two days, Bill needed more rest in bed. When released from the hospital he headed straight back to the Conradt's house to heal. The Conradt family was fast becoming his family.

Bill lay around in Fred's room while his lacerated head mended. He sketched by the hour and was delighted to have Alice for a frequent visitor. She was shy about visiting him at first, but was irresistibly drawn to him. When Bill told her about his life as a lone cowboy, about Old Beaupre being his only family, and about his desire to become an artist like Charlie Russell, that did the trick. They let themselves fall in love.

Will James takes Alice for a ride on his new Bools and Butler saddle. Note 26"
tapaderos. (circa 1919). — Courtesy Clint and Donna Conradt, all rights reserved.

116

During 'Will James' Dufault's youth, he dreamed of wandering over the Western landscape. When he reached the age of fifteen his dream became a reality. Bill had roamed the West for many years, and now he suddenly had a craving for something more than a good horse and saddle. He wanted this fair-haired woman.

Another emotion was also surfacing inside Bill, an emotion that gnawed at him constantly. He wasn't satisfied with being a cowboy any longer; he wanted more. He knew the time had arrived for him to make a try at becoming a successful artist.

Charlie Russell in his log cabin studio at Great Falls, Montana. He was probably the only artist whose work Will James respected and admired. — Montana Historical Society, Helena.

Bill knew that achieving the status of a professional artist would not be easy, for no matter how many try, only a few succeed. In the beginning he was aware that art is creating the spirit of a subject in a tangible form and it cannot be done for money alone. It means believing in the subject so completely that it becomes alive in the artist's mind.

Even an intelligent, multi-talented artist like Will James had to

117

pay his dues before reaching a level of maturity in his work that would ensure its acceptance by the public.

Bill told Alice of a time not long ago when he had stopped over in Great Falls, Montana, to see the artist "all the cowboys knowed." He described the hurt he'd felt when he showed some of his drawings to Charlie Russell and the artist was unimpressed. Bill told Alice this man was a real cowboy. "He had the whole map of the cow country on his face," Bill explained. The following letter explains Bill's first meeting with Charlie Russell.

Anthony Amaral   May 26, 1961
Cal-Poly Stables
POMONA
CALIFORNIA

Dear Tony:

I was under such pressure the week of the Rancheros that the reaction has pretty-well layed me out. In any case, I've done little other than *sleep* since my return home, the 15th.

Even so, I have nothing of interest to pass along other than to answer your question in regard to Will James' visit to Russell's studio. (As far as I know, he only made one such, and did not meet Russell again until after his (Bill's) illustrated articles that appeared in *Sunset Magazine* attracted nationwide attention. This next meeting having been in New York — I think; though they spent some time in each other's company, out here, one or two winters later on.) I know for sure that they got together at Harry Carey's Ranch. Also that Russell, James, Ed Borein and Will Rogers went to a calf-branding together, somewhere up around Livermore — about 1923.

As for James' visit to Russell's studio: I seem unable to recall the year, but am certain it was between 1917 and '20. In any case, he just happened to drop in when Russell was bogged down in one of his extremely-rare, deeply-absorbed moods wherein he was almost completely "lost" from anything and anybody around him; a state of mind that his wife and a few close friends understood, and either accepted as commonplace or joked about. As a result, in this particular instance, his general attitude and his answers to Bill's questions and remarks were sort of an absent-minded mumble (as near as I can discribe my own impression) since he was deeply absorbed in a picture that hadn't been going right. As a result, Bill assumed that he received something in the nature of a brush-off; which I sensed, and in fact took the trouble to follow him outside, as he left, and tried to explain the matter. However, his drawing, together with his discription of this incident in Lone Cowboy, indicated that he believed Russell's attitude was a matter of personal indifference.

Yours,

Joe De Yong

Special Collections Department, University of Nevada Reno Library.

As the lonesome cowboy healed, he and Alice cemented their relationship. Alice wanted him to quit riding broncs and enter into art full time. Bill felt his throbbing head and considered this a good idea. The two lovers worked out a plan.

Bill was notoriously lazy when he wasn't a-horseback. The industrious 'Pappa' Conradt picked up on this trait right away and voiced his opinion to his wife, Mary Conradt. However, 'Mamma' liked Bill and defended him openly. Bill and Alice speculated that going to art school was now the best move Bill could make. It would help him open doors in the art world and prove to the Conradts he was striving to be more than just a loafing cowboy.

Bill made arrangements to go to San Francisco and enroll in the California School of Fine Arts. He hocked his saddle for train fare. On a warm August morning Mrs. Conradt and all of her brood came to see their favorite cowboy artist off on his trip to California. Bill kissed the tear-stained face of Alice and jumped onto the steps of the moving train. His two friends, Fred and Elmer, pushed their way through and handed him what money they had left.

"I cain't take this from you fellers," Bill argued.

"Hell, take it, Bill," Fred argued right back at him. "You know where we'd spend it anyhow."

In San Francisco Bill found a room in a small hotel. He registered for evening classes at the art school, and because his funds were limited he took a job as an usher in a nearby movie theater. Only a short time later he came to the profound conclusion that the standard formula for a Hollywood western was two dozen cowboys; four dozen guns; six teepees full of Indians; three bad guys; one mortgage; one hero (brave); and one girl (sweet). He developed a theory that as a subject, the real cowboy's West made quite as good a story as the phony shoot-'em-ups, and folks might even learn from the true story. He said many times that Hollywood would be willing to accept the real thing, the working cowboy's story, if it were properly presented.

Bill settled into his routine of morning art practice, his matinee usher job, and school in the evening.

"One afternoon I was a guest of one of the instructors at the art school," Lee Rice, a well-known California artist, explained in 1960 as he recalled those early years when he met Bill. "While viewing the work of the class I came to a small, bowlegged fellow wearing cowboy boots. On his sheet of drawing paper was a very poor attempt at a drawing of the model, but on the margin were several fine drawings of cowboys and horses in violent action. These drawings were the source of many headaches to his instructors as they strived to impart the finer points of art to this cowboy who seemed interested only in cowboys and horses. I was wearing cowboy boots and that, coupled with my keen interest in the horse sketches, caused James to quickly recognize me as a fellow traveler from the sagebrush country. From this initial meeting grew a long and lasting friendship."

A few days after his meeting with Bill, Lee invited the cowboy to visit the studio of his lifelong friend and one of the truly great Western painters, Maynard Dixon.

Dixon reviewed Bill's cow country sketches and advised him to quit art school immediately. It was Dixon's contention that if Bill

120

Will James and Fred Conradt discussing the finer points of horsemanship. When in the city James ardently missed the company of a horse.

continued in art school it would ruin his work, for he had a free style of drawing. He never made a preliminary sketch, but drew directly from a clear concept he had in his mind, and he completed the drawing as he progressed. This crisp technique would be destroyed if Bill continued with art school. Dixon told Bill that what he needed was work, to draw ten thousand horses but to do it in his own style. Bill's quick climb to success may well prove that Maynard Dixon's advice was another of the important turning points in his life.

Bill quit art school and worked diligently on his drawings in the dingy little hotel on lower Mission Street. During this period he made several friends who were concerned about his welfare and believed in his work, friends such as Lee Rice, Maynard Dixon, Harold Von Schmidt, art director for Foster and Kleiser advertising firm, and Charlie Duncan, sales department manager for the same firm.

His friends talked him into moving to Sausalito, and later a couple of them drove the lonely cowboy to a livestock sales yard south of Market Street. They walked over to a corral full of horses and told Bill to pick one out. He wasted no time in putting a halter on a good-looking iron-grey gelding with dapples sprinkled over its legs and hips. Harold Von Schmidt loaned him a saddle. Having a horse to ride made Bill feel better, and the results of these good feelings showed in his work.

Von Schmidt described two of the drawings he saw during his first meeting with Bill when the cowboy dropped by to visit at his office.

> I asked him about the little package he carried under his arm. He unwrapped it, showing me two shoebox bottoms. On each he had drawn minutely everything that could go on at a cattle ranch — in one corner was a ranch house with horses tied to a rail in front, the rest was filled with one corral where they were branding calves; in another they were breaking horses, in the next they were shoeing them, on the other side they were bringing herds in, and below taking a herd out. In another picture they were cutting calves from the cows through a swinging gate operated by a man sitting on it. I was fascinated by the drawings and hoped to buy them later.
>
> — Ed Ainsworth, *The Cowboy In Art*,
> World Publishing Company, 1968.

Bill's friends pulled some more strings, and when he walked into the offices of Sunset magazine, ". . .with the tang of sagebrush still clinging to him," he carried his hopes in a portfolio of drawings. When he left he carried a check in his hand.

After finishing four or five drawings for Sunset, he did a series of four drawings illustrating the life of "Keno, the Cow Horse." The drawings showed the growing-up stages of a colt through its first four years until it was old enough to be broken as a cowhorse. Bill wrote the three-paragraph introduction to the series, the first time his writing appeared in print.

Keno, the Cow-Horse

A Life-Story in Pictures

By Will James

TO my way of thinking the little old cow-horse is the only animal that can be banked on, that's really a feller's friend. He will pack you out of trouble and pick the way for you when you aint able. He's got four good legs under him, and a good set of brains. He will make you like him if you're worth it, and while he's got no use for a master, he sure appreciates a man.

Many a time when I used to sashay out on the horse range and haze in a bunch of horses I'd watch the colts as they picked their way over the rocky trail to the water hole or skip pretty like round the catclaws and cactus. I used to kinda try and figure out what sort of a horse was going to come of some particular little feller I'd see running round and shying at something he'd just imagine was there when it wasn't.

Keno, in his prime, was sure a great little cow-horse, from the time he first smelled saddle-leather until he was pensioned after he done his best for the company. I watched him from the day he was born and saw him through to the end. So I've put Keno here in these pictures, from one end of his life to the other—just one of the thousands of his kind that folks outside the cow countries never hear about, but a great little horse all the same.

WILL JAMES

Sunset (November, 1920).
Courtesy A.P. Hays.

With the obvious exception of horses, Will James' initial love was art and he had no ambition to become a writer when he arrived in San Francisco. Bill was, however, a natural storyteller. Sunset's associate editor, Joseph Henry Jackson, had recognized his potential and now urged him to write and illustrate stories about some of his range experiences for the magazine. Bill had gone no farther than the third grade in school and the suggestion bothered him. Jackson knew that Bill had a wealth of story material in him, and he believed if the cowboy forgot about grammar and wrote as he talked, his words would be entertaining to the reading public. This advice by Joseph Henry Jackson became the basis of another important turning point in the life and success of Will James.

Overcoming the challenges in a creative field has never been easy. It has been said that every success story was built on a monumental pile of failures.

Bill accepted the fact of hard work, and he was prepared to meet the challenge head on, but he felt incomplete and lonesome. In July, 1920, the twenty-eight-year-old Bill took time out from his busy schedule to return to Reno and shortly thereafter was married to sixteen-year-old Alice.

Alice was one of the good things in Bill's life. Through the ups and downs of his personal and business life she was always there. The lone cowboy now had a family to whom he belonged.

Bill and Alice migrated from Reno, Nevada, to Sausalito, California, on to Kingman, Arizona, and finally wound up in Santa Fe, New Mexico. At Santa Fe Bill had a little spurt of success in selling art but eventually went broke.

Ed Springer, rancher, Will James benefactor. — Special Collections Department, University of Nevada Reno Library.

His funds exhausted, Bill turned to his old profession of riding and applied for a job on a nearby ranch, the Springer Ranch. On that high-country cow outfit Bill met a man who became a benefactor of the struggling artist. Ed Springer hired Bill, but he arranged a schedule in the cow camp so that Bill would have time to work on his drawings.

Burt Twitchell, Dean of Students at Yale University, benefactor of Will James. — Special Collections Department, University of Nevada Reno Library.

A stronger influence on Bill's life, however, came from a visitor to this ranch, Burton Twitchell, dean of students at Yale University. Twitchell became acquainted with Bill around campfires on his annual deer-hunting trip to New Mexico. As a result of this association with Twitchell, Bill went to New York for an attempt at launching his career in the large eastern markets.

That fleeting, elusive thing called success always seemed to be right around the corner. Bill illustrated working cowboys in their natural environments, and he could not understand why those eastern publishers chose "shoot-'em-up" illustrations over his work.

Alice traveled back to Reno. She rented an apartment on the Coughlin ranch west of town along the Truckee River. When Bill returned to Nevada, smarting from wounds to his professional pride, he was delighted with the new set-up, but he missed his old friends, the One-Elevens.

Bill was surprised to find that Fred had married Dolly, his sweetheart from California. Fred and Dolly had moved to the Walker Lake country, where Fred was manager of a cattle ranch.

The One-Elevens in a wrestling match. Will James was to miss such fun-loving days with his "ol' buddies."

Earlier that year Elmer had married a lady bronc rider and moved to California. The hell-raising bachelor days of the One-Elevens were now a memory.

Bill missed his old buddies, but the everyday routine on the Coughlin ranch was pleasant to him, and he was able to settle in. He applied himself completely to his work, in mind, spirit, and body.

Alice wanted Bill to write stories even before their marriage, but he'd always argued against it. Now he began to reconsider. Bill felt he was failing at other pursuits and suddenly he told Alice he was willing to give writing a try. She wanted him to write stories of authentic cowboy lore using the language of a working cowboy. "You should write about bucking horses," she said, "because that's all you want to talk about!"

Bill threw his hands in the air, muttered a few words, and began writing. Alice worried about pushing Bill too hard, and her younger sister Agnes also warned her about pressuring Bill. At first he wouldn't say anything; he simply withdrew from Alice, but the resentment came out when he drank.

A few weeks later, Bill handed Alice a manuscript written in longhand with several illustrations. He asked her to mail the package to Scribner's magazine.

Bill had written the story exactly the way he would have told it to cowboys on the roundup as they loafed around a campfire. He had no expectations of selling the article, since he could not imagine an eastern publishing firm wanting to publish anything written in true Western jargon. He could see no similarity in his work to any of the magazine articles or books currently being published about the West. Bill had no way of knowing that this difference, rather than stating mediocrity, made his story an exceptional piece of regional writing.

In a relatively short time Bill received an acceptance letter from Scribner's and a check. At first he couldn't believe his eyes and he reread the letter several times. *Bucking Horses and Bucking Horse Riders* appeared in Scribner's magazine in 1922, and from that time to the present, Will James' work has been in print.

Bill isolated himself and went into an intensive work period. He labored around the clock with only cat naps to keep him going. Through necessity in his earlier years, the lone cowboy had developed a self-sustaining, independent nature which had always seen him through such times. His bride found this condition hard to live with though, because she was in love and wanted to be with her husband.

Scribner's easily accepted the next illustrated article, *A Cowpuncher Speaks*. Bill later learned that his first article about bucking horses had bogged down in Scribner's editorial department because of the cowboy jargon, but the art department thought his illustrations were exceptional and insisted on the story being used.

The Saturday Evening Post purchased *Pinon and the Wild Ones*, an illustrated story about trapping mustangs. *Sunset* magazine bought a three-part article called *Bronc Twisters*, and *Redbook* magazine requested an article. Bill had shown such enthusiasm on this new enterprise of writing that his work surpassed both his and Alice's expectations. His career was elevated to that enviable position of having buyers for his work before it was completed. Hard times came to an end for Mr. and Mrs. James.

Bill figured he could handle success just fine. He could spend money right along with the rest of them. He took Alice and headed for Reno. They walked into the first car lot they saw and picked out the biggest car on the lot. Bill kicked the tires, honked the horn, and then asked the salesman the price. He nodded, paid the man, and told Alice to hop in. It never occurred to Alice to ask Bill if he knew how to drive.

Bill climbed into the driver's seat as the automobile sat idling. He found reverse and backed out, much in the manner of a wild, stampeding bronc coming out of a chute. The 1920 Pierce Arrow shot across the street like an arrow and smashed into a telephone pole on the opposite side. The car sputtered a few times and then, fortunately, the engine stalled.

A pale-faced Bill turned to a paler-faced Alice, "God-a-mighty!" he gasped, "I think I spurred it too hard!"

The range of magazines for which Bill supplied illustrated articles increased rapidly. In October, 1924, several of his stories were put together in a book by Scribner's. *Cowboys North and South* was readily accepted by an eager public, and the critics praised it highly. The New York Herald Tribune wrote, "What he says is worth listening to. What he draws is even more gorgeous. Mr. James has done a magnificent book."

. . .

The black Pierce Arrow with its red leather upholstery and chrome trim sped down the road at 35 miles per hour as it left the Reno city limits and headed south. On each side of the road were irrigated pasturelands of the Truckee meadows. Steam billowed out of the ground, and the smell of sulfur drifted through the windows of the Pierce as it wheeled past Steamboat Springs and over a low pass in the hills. Off to the left was Washoe Lake, with hundreds of cattle grazing around its green borders and flocks of ducks and geese dotting its surface.

The James Cabin in Washoe Valley, Nevada, looks much the same today as it did when it was first built by the Conradts in 1923. — Courtesy Gwendolyn Clancy.

There were a few houses along the road to the left, and the large estate of Bowers Mansion on the right. Soon the Pierce was cruising through a forest; huge ponderosa pines were all around, and a thick carpet of pine needles spread under the stately trees. Bill turned to the right into a lane, past a corral with three horses in it, and braked to a stop in front of a newly constructed log house. He crawled out from behind the wheel and walked around to help Alice out of the car. His arm encircled his wife as the two walked toward their new home.

"Your Pappa and brothers did one hellacious good job building this house," Bill told her.

People grow old and die, but the solid, log house stands in Washoe Valley today looking much the same as when it was first built by that sturdy German immigrant in 1923.

Once the couple settled into their new home, Bill plunged into a rigorous work schedule. He had a small studio built behind the new house. Each morning he strolled down to the corral to feed the horses. He would roll and smoke a few twirlys and watch the three cowponies eat, then go directly to his studio. He left orders that no one, not even Alice, was to disturb him when he was working.

Alice was lonesome in this idyllic setting. Some days she wouldn't see Bill for twenty-four hours at a time. She spent much of her time by herself, going for walks or riding on trails that meandered through pine-clad mountains behind their house. When Bill first started writing he often asked her opinion about such things as sentence structure, spelling, or story ideas, but now he refused to consult her. She never knew what he was writing until it appeared in print.

Elmer Freel died suddenly, and Bill dropped the III from his signature. Bill felt bad about losing his old friend, and he and Alice were happy Fred accepted a job as foreman on a nearby ranch. After Fred and Dolly moved closer things were better for Alice. The two couples enjoyed occasional horseback rides, and they traveled to rodeos, stock fairs, and autograph parties for Bill.

Bill had a new book in print, *The Drifting Cowboy*, another collection of short stories. It was critically treated to the grand compliments that were bestowed on his first book. Bookman magazine described the illustrations as "vigorously alive as a young bronc on a frosty morning." A critic in Outlook magazine wrote, "Will James

Dolly, Fred, and Alice enjoyed frequent horseback rides in the Washoe Valley while Will James was "holed-up" in his studio writing Smoky. — Courtesy Clint and Donna Conradt, all rights reserved.

has a distinct literary style. He has that and more and Scribner's have had the good judgement not to translate the book into English."

When Bill had completed his first book, *Cowboys North and South*, he received a letter from Scribner's Editor, Maxwell Perkins. Perkins suggested that Bill write a continuous narrative with a plot. He felt the time was right because of the public's acceptance of Bill's work.

Bill went to work on the idea immediately. For a year he labored over the book and its illustrations. He detached himself from Alice, Fred, and Dolly for long periods of seclusion, then one day strolled into the living room and proudly announced to them, "I jest finished the book on my 'ol Smoky hoss."

As in his other books, Bill wrote *Smoky* in the vernacular of the Western cowboy, using his everyday speech in an easy loping kind of style. This writing as people actually talked was later popularized by fiction writers like Ernest Hemingway and John Steinbeck. Bill did it effortlessly in *Smoky*, and the book is composed with consummate art.

Like many of the "bowlegged fellers," Bill wrote out of passion rather than intellect. He was able to give to others, through his work, an intense feeling of participation in the cowboy's way of life as it was staged in the wild and windswept world known as the West.

Of all the words written about horse culture, Will James' work stands supreme. He will always be the bowlegged genius who illustrated in drawings and words the most exciting horses folks will see in their lifetimes. The drawings and paintings in *Smoky The Cowhorse* are some of his finest. The painting of a young Smoky and a bay horse named Pecos fighting a big black horse is indeed one of a kind. The drawing of Smoky while he is in the hackamore after Clint has roped a sagebrush and it is flying toward the colt, spooking him, is a wonderful piece of creative art. The drawing that can give a person goosebumps, however, is the drawing of "The Cougar," Smoky turned outlaw. Bill's words described the incident pictured

"Fights for rights."

"Smoky starts out."

The Cougar.

Illustrations from *Smoky The Cowhorse*.

Will James, SMOKEY THE COWHORSE, copyright © 1926 Charles Scribner's Sons; copyright renewed 1961 Auguste Dufault. Reprinted with the permission of Charles Scribner's Sons.

in the drawing: "The Cougar reared up while the rider was still in the air. He turned, and with ears back, teeth a flashing, hoofs a striking with lightning speed, went on to carry out his hearts craving."

In the black and white illustration, everything Bill describes is mirrored in that horse's face.

> As an illustrator, particularly of the horse, James is supreme. The horse, as the land itself, was always a surging emotion for him and, unlike his feelings for the land, he could express the power, symmetry and beauty of the horse. By a gleam in its eye, position of an ear, or the dilation of the nostrils, James vividly showed a horse's fear, rage, alertness and, no less powerful, a horse in peaceful repose. A horse could not contort itself into any position that James was unable to photograph in his mind and reproduce that image on paper. Whether in pen and ink, brush and ink, stump and charcoal, or in oils, James' talent breathed life into his horses with an accurate flow of lines. His ease and sponteneity in drawing were a great gift, and as the critics have noted: 'for perfect expression of muscle packed energy, James' broncs are inimitable. . .' His horses seem to leap from the page and kick dirt all over you. . .
>
> — Anthony Amaral, *The Gilt Edged Cowboy*,
> Westernlore Press, 1967

Creative people are driven by their motivations. Without a doubt the strongest motivation in the entire life of Will James was his love for horses. The true genius of the man lay in painting and writing about horses. He had compassion for these animals and an understanding of what goes on between their ears, for a horse's way of thinking is entirely different from the way other animals think, especially the human animal. Bill never humanized his horses. When one of the cowboys in his books was through using a horse, he turned the animal loose and left it alone. Bill understood how a horse in its natural environment needed to live, and he respected the horse for being simply a natural animal.

Modern-day buckaroos show the influence of the old-time cowboys in their dress and lifestyle. 00 Ranch, Seligman, Arizona. — Photo by Kurt Markus © 1987.

Because of his ability to describe the way he felt for horses, Bill's books have always been popular with young readers and Westerners in general. In the 1980s it is becoming apparent that there is much more at work here. Buckaroos working on ranches around the West are avid fans of Bill's writing and artwork, to the point of patterning their lives after him.

The strong realism of Will James' illustrations depicting fights among men, broncos, and wild cattle, can be unappealing to gentle, indoor people. But Bill is an insider's artist, and cowboys are attracted to their real-life hero and his work. Will James, not Russell or Remington, is the favorite of the cowboy.

> . . . Will James came riding like a cowboy into a Ladies Aid meeting. The impact of his arrival was all the more dramatic

because it was so unexpected. The same generation that had been brought up on the pap of 'Black Beauty,' a steed so genteel he presumably used cologne, suddenly was confronted with 'Smoky,' an honest-to-God range horse with guts and a hell of a lot of earthy character. 'Smoky' captivated America.

— Ed Ainsworth, *The Cowboy in Art*,
World Publishing Company, 1968

On two good horses, all merry and full off cheer
We wish you a fine Christmas and a Happy New Year
Alice & Bill James
'31

Will James, *The Drifting Cowboy* — Jim Bramlett

In Lone Cowboy, Will James wrote that he had drifted from Canada to Mexico and back on his "ol' Smoky Hoss," with a good gray packhorse trailing behind.

Will James and wife Alice on the
porch of their log house in
Washoe Valley, Nevada, where
Smoky The Cowhorse *was
created.* (circa 1925). — Courtesy Clint and
Donna Conradt, all rights reserved.

Chapter V

THE ONE AND ONLY SMOKY

*"I haven't been on a horse for three months which shows how
I'm working. I'm trying to better my stories and there's so much I
have to learn on it every way but I'm afraid if I get too careful it'll
be just like in my pictures and that is I'll lose the swing I try to put
in. I find I have the best out when I go at it wild and reckless, sling
things all directions and put 'em together rough. But I'm not at all
set in my ideas, I've always got my ears and eyes a working for
whatever will better what I do."*

— Excerpt from a letter to Burt Twitchell
from Will James, 1923

137

SMOKY
THE COW HORSE

Written and Illustrated
by WILL JAMES

Smoky The Cowhorse, *by Will James,*
first published in 1926.

SMOKY WAS A VITAL ELEMENT in Will James' life, and quite possibly the most important. *Smoky* has been in print continuously since 1926. No biography of Will James could be complete without a segment devoted to that smoke-colored horse, and so, for all the readers who haven't read the book or haven't read it for awhile, here's a short introduction to the beginning of this story.

> It seemed like Mother Nature was sure agreeable that day when the little black colt came into the range world and tried to get a footing with his long wobblety legs on the brown prairie sod. Short stems of new, green grass was trying to make their way up through the last year's faded growth and reaching for the sun's warm rays. Taking in all that could be seen, felt and inhaled, there was no day, time nor place that could beat that spring morning on the sunny side of the low prairie butte where Smoky the colt was foaled.

These are the opening words of the most beautiful and poignant story ever written about horses in the range country. The story is simple, but the details are rich and absorbing. It is a realistic account of a working cow pony during the days before World War I,

138

back when most of the terrain from the Great Plains to the Pacific Ocean was livestock country. It was a world of cows, horses, and leather-covered men with singing spurs.

In those days, a man's pride was in the calibre of horse he rode. Even on ranches today a cowboy is frequently judged by the horse he is riding and how that rider can bring out the horse's class and form at working cows. A horse's class is the degree of trained ability he possesses. His form is the positioning to maintain control over livestock, but remain light on the rein and supple for the rider. With such a horse, working stock is not only pleasurable but most expedient.

In California and Nevada good stock horses are described as horses that stop in one movement with their noses tucked in; turn with their front feet off the ground; and can be jumped out at any angle the rider wants to take. They stop straight and can turn halfway or spin, and they do it easily. When sorting cows on the cutting grounds they drop their heads and, on a slack rein, throw themselves around to block a cow.

To show this kind of athletic performance a horse has to be strong, fast, and agile. There are a few good, finished horses around, but horsemen are always searching for the one new colt that promises to be special.

Will James' Smoky is something special. He is an intelligent animal that puts his heart and soul into living. Bill describes Smoky

Cattle being held on the cutting grounds where cowboys ride into the herd to do the sorting. L.A. Huffman photo. (circa 1915) — Montana Historical Society, Helena.

139

as a mouse-colored gelding, and that's how he pictures him in his paintings, a grulla with four white socks, and a blaze face.

Smoky is from range stock. Will James says Smoky is mustang with strains of Steeldust thrown in. The mustang blood that flows though his veins makes him tough. Generations of wild horses that fought the lobo and the cougar instilled in Smoky instincts of a fighter, and the Steeldust blood gave him the size and speed to do a good job of it.

Bill's description of a starry-eyed little colt growing up in open range country is a beautiful piece of work. It is a story that could only be told by someone who has spent many years studying horses in their natural environment. From the first time the colt nurses to its scrape with a hungry coyote, the early months are filled with adventure. The curious colt investigates each new critter it encounters in the mountainous country and is always on the lookout for something new to spook at, giving it another excuse to burn the breeze at a dead run. More important, Bill describes in detail how the colt fits into a social order of the range horse.

The first summer of Smoky's life the herd ranges high to escape the heat and flies. Mountain grass is greener than the grass down below and along with trees for shade, things are nice and peaceful, until a rider appears on a ridge above them. The little bunch of horses goes into action simultaneously. They race across a bench and down the mountain at a dead run with the rider trailing along behind. Tails a-popping, the horses sail over rocks and ledges, slide down soft, sandy spots, and leap across washouts. The rocks and soft dirt loosened by the surging herd roll down the mountain, crashing into boulders and dead hanging timber, causing a small avalanche of dirt and slash.

The running herd, followed by the lone rider, passes through the canyon and speed across the flat toward the ranch headquarters.

The range horses are driven into a large corral with many others of their kind. Most of the older horses are cut out of the bunch and pushed into a smaller corral, leaving all the colts with a few gentle mares. Smoky crowds into the herd and manages to hide behind an

old mare. As he peers out from under her belly, trying to get a look at his first human being, he is pertrified at what he sees: a strange-looking creature that stands on its hind legs. The creature makes a sweeping motion with one paw and suddenly there is fire in its hand. Soon Smoky sees smoke coming out of the creature's mouth. This is spooky business to a colt!

Smoky's eyes are blazing as he watches one of the bowlegged cowboys pick up a rope and walk toward him. The horses tear around the corral and raise a lot of dust. The human gives the rope a flip to one side, then shoots it out with the speed of a lightning bolt. Smoky sees the loop roll out and wrap around the front legs of a charging colt. The colt squeals in terror and is soon tied down. Smoky can't bear to watch anymore; he whirls around and tries to melt into the horse bunch.

Smoky dodges and hides out the best he can, but soon it is apparent to him that there are no safe places. Those cowboys are everywhere with their long ropes reaching out all around him. He is circling for the outside of the bunch when he hears a rope hiss close by and something coils around his own front legs. In no time at all he is flat on the ground with all four feet tied up.

When it is all over, his legs are untied and with a gentle pat on his fanny to boost him along his way, he trots off. He has been castrated and is wearing a neat little brand that will be a part of him for the rest of his life, the Rocking R brand. After the colts are all branded they are turned in with their mammies to mother-up. The gate is opened and soon the horses are drifting back to the high mountain range.

The book, *Smoky*, elaborates on the experiences of the colt as it finishes out the summer, how its mammy weans it that fall, and how Smoky goes on to spend the winter pawing for snow to get at the good grass underneath. Bill's description of the everyday range life of the colt is very special. He delights in relating how the colt stays in good flesh all winter and has daily romps in the snow. The weanling grows long winter hair to keep it warm when the blizzards blow. Being a privileged character, Smoky moves in on some of the big horses with ears laid back and runs them away from the grass they had recently pawed for. Of course, the adult horses are only acting scared to humor the colt.

Smoky's first winter wears on, and finally spring comes. The snow begins to melt. The horses' blood hasn't thinned yet, and they become sluggish and lazy. As soon as new sprouts of green grass appear, things change rapidly for the range horses. They won't touch the old brown grass they had pawed for all winter and will only chase the new stuff. This does the trick, and although the horses lose weight, their blood thins down and they begin to shed chunks of old winter hair.

Smoky's winter coat fades to brown. As he rolls on warm, dry spots on the southern slopes of the hills he leaves a lot of old hair, which allows his new color to show through. It starts to show a mousy-gray color on his head and flanks and finally all over his body. He has a small head for his size and is one of those good kinds of ponies with a short back and long underline. His lengthy legs are set under him for balance and quickness.

The most important thing that happens to Smoky during his second summer is the arrival of his little brother. When that little colt shows up, Smoky immediately ranks second in the horse herd, but this doesn't bother him one little bit. He figures he has the world by the tail in a downhill pull, and he becomes so strong-minded and full of mischief that the other horses realize they'll have to put him in his place with a lot of biting and kicking.

The mouse-colored colt grows up, and as he is beginning his third year a big change takes place. It happens one sunny afternoon as he

142

The range stallion is boss of his herd and is always willing to fight to prove it. Courtesy Bureau of Land Management.

is trailing along with the little bunch on the way to a watering hole. The peaceful monotony is shattered from "hell to breakfast," for there in the middle of the trail is a big, black range stud.

In a natural state, the stallion is boss and leader of the herd as long as he can fight off any other males who might try to take over the leadership of the band of mares and colts. The herd is loyal to him only during the time he can maintain this supremacy against all newcomers. Like the bull elk, a stallion is polygamous and will fight to take any female he can win over. It is the classic example of survival of the fittest, nature's way of limiting reproduction to the strongest.

The stud's herd of mares and colts watches from the background as "that black cloud of horseflesh" moves into Smoky's bunch. As soon as the stallion learns there is no herd stud, he goes to work getting things adjusted to his way of thinking. In a businesslike manner he cuts the geldings out of the herd. Smoky hadn't planned on leaving his mammy so suddenly, and he fights back. However, he hadn't reckoned with the fighting qualities of a range stallion either. The hair flies, and when it is over Smoky is running full speed up country while the stallion takes the mares, including Smoky's mammy, and goes on down the country.

Smoky and an old retired buckskin gelding bum around the range

143

together until Smoky becomes a long four-year-old. The two geldings join up with another bunch of horses and are getting fat as they graze on the mountainside.

The muscles ripple under his hide as Smoky rims around the mountain to get at the more succulent bunches of grass. As the afternoon sun is sparkling off his healthy, seal-fat hide, the mouse-colored gelding is easy for a Rocking R cowboy to study through binoculars. The man utters a low whistle at the sight of this good-looking horse.

That evening at the ranch the cowboy tells Clint, the bronc buster for the outfit, about seeing the grulla colt and where it is ranging. A few days later that same horse breaker appears on a ridge above the little bunch, and off they go. Many miles away the bunch is penned in big cottonwood log corrals. Smoky is cut out of the bunch and run into another corral full of geldings his own age, and the rest of the herd is turned back on the range. They don't linger one little bit as Smoky nickers to them.

Smoky watches through the corral bars as the bunch disappears in a cloud of dust. If it wasn't for those bars, he could catch up in no time. Suddenly he hears the gate squeak and whirls around to face the human.

Clint walks into the corral, a coiled rope on his arm. As he stands there rolling a smoke, he watches the pacing, nervous colt. Just looking at that chunk of mouse-colored horseflesh makes Clint feel good all over.

When a horse herd is turned out they "don't let any grass grow under their feet" as they "hightail it" back to their range. (circa 1928) — Courtesy Clint and Donna Conradt, all rights reserved.

144

"Smoky," he says, "you are some kind of a horse." Clint is so intent on studying the moves of the little horse that he doesn't realize he just named the four-year-old, and the name fits. Smoky does look like a cloud of gray smoke.

Clint had started the breaking and training of eighty head of horses during the two years he had worked for that outfit. He takes ten horses at a time. After he gets the rough edge off these colts and has them coming around a little, he turns them over to the regular riders, and starts another bunch of raw wild ones.

Clint had started horses for many outfits before this one, and the effects of all that rough action is beginning to tell on him. He had been laid up many times with broken bones, some of which hadn't mended the way they should. He had begun to feel like an old man at thirty.

Horses are the important element of Clint's life. He started cowboying as a "young'un" and was a top hand when he reached maturity. Clint knows the time is approaching when he'll have to draw the line on riding broncs. He plans to stop riding the rough string, but he's been waiting a long time for the right kind of horse to come

Fred Conradt on his top horse, a "bald-faced" grulla he called Keno (circa 1931) — Courtesy Clint and Donna Conradt, all rights reserved.

145

along first, and here it is in the shape of a mouse-colored bronc he calls Smoky.

The more Clint looks at the horse, the more he wants him for his own. Smoky is the kind of horse Clint has been searching for all his life. The gelding belongs to the Rocking R outfit, of course, but Clint is making plans to get that animal for himself somehow.

Every evening, after finishing with the last meal of the day, Clint goes down to see Smoky. He spends many days on the ground making friends with that pony before he decides to ride him. Clint does this on his own because he wouldn't have thought it honest to spend company time to slowly gentle a horse. He uses care and patience to break Smoky, compared to the standard old-time method in which a bronc buster "ties up a hind foot, sacks 'em out, blindfolds 'em, saddles 'em, climbs on, raises the blind and lets 'em unwind."

In other parts of the country there were bronc riders who would whip a colt each time it bucked. Some of those old-time *vaqueros* could sit up there in a slick fork saddle and pop a colt on the end of the nose with a quirt every time that bronc hit the ground. The idea behind this was to improve the bronc by making it afraid to buck. When they quit bucking and threw up their heads, the whipping stopped.

How many horses Will James broke and trained no one will ever know, but in his description of Clint's step-by-step procedure it's obvious that Bill has been there many times before. He goes into detail about how Clint leads Smoky into the round corral and sacks him out with an old saddle blanket. The word pictures he paints in describing Smoky's reaction to the sacking-out and the horse's first saddling give the reader a clear picture of what is going on in that corral and in the horse's mind.

The real excitement begins when Clint first rides the mouse-colored horse. He pulls the latigo, and as the cinch tightens around Smoky's belly a hump appears in the pony's back. Clint doesn't lead him around to settle the hump because he is one of those cowboys who tries especially hard to keep a horse's spirit intact while break-

146

ing him. Clint believes any horse worth its salt should buck when ridden the first few times. Smoky doesn't disappoint him in that respect. During the first saddling, Smoky bucks wild and scared. The second saddling is much harder. The horse is smart and has a plan of action worked out for getting his man. The third saddling is a repeat of the second. Clint admires the horse even more for the way he uses his brain to try to shed the rider.

Smoky's bucking tapers off after the third go-round, and Clint takes him outside on daily rides where he ropes sagebrush and limbs off trees and even drags logs around. The cowboy enjoys watching the way Smoky is adjusting to all these new lessons. Smoky's little ears move back and forth, aware of everything that goes on.

Clint rides the colt into a bunch of cows and plays with them, then ropes a calf or two. This suits Smoky just fine because he likes to chase the wild-eyed cow and turn her when she doesn't want to be turned. Smoky enjoys the evening rides when he can play with the tall, slim rider on his back.

Two months pass from the time of their first meeting in the round corral. The wild horse and the cowboy'd had some tough fights, but in all those battles the man had won. As Smoky gains confidence in this cowboy, he begins to nicker at the man and goes the length of his picket rope to meet him. Each time he is ridden, however, the bronc has to have his little bucking session.

Clint quits the rough string and goes with the wagon on the cattle roundup, and the Rocking R cowboss allows him to take the smoke-colored bronc with him. The beginning days on roundup are exciting times for Smoky, not unlike a kid's first days in school. He is turned into a remuda of two hundred head of saddle horses. When camp is moved, the wagons roll across the prairie at a walk, then a trot, and when the teams hit a high lope all the rattling and banging makes those colts feel spooky and frisky, and they playfully kick up their heels.

When the pilot raises a hand the wagons circle and a camp is made on the spot. The cook wastes no time in getting a fire going under the dutch ovens, and soon a rope corral is strung up and the remuda run in.

Temporary corrals were commonly formed in the shape of a 'U' by using a heavy rope, called a cable, held three feet off the ground by men or by stakes driven into the ground. This looks seemingly frail for a bunch of horses, but early in life the cowhorse learns to respect a rope. If a new horse breaks out of the corral, the cowboss gives a nod to one of the riders to rope him and "pick up his toes."

As soon as the cowboys have their mounts caught they drop the cable and the remuda is allowed to return to their grazing. Everything is done as quietly as possible. Having performed its duty, the cable is coiled and placed in the wagon to be ready for the next change of horses.

The rope corral is a mobile "ketch pen" used on roundup. It is a heavy rope cable held three feet off the ground by stakes driven into the ground. (circa 1930)
— Courtesy Clint and Donna Conradt, all rights reserved.

148

Leather-covered range riders going to the roundup. L.A. Huffman photo, (circa 1915) — Montana Historical Society, Helena.

The Rocking R cowboys handily put away the noon "bait" of beef, beans, and bisquits and go to the rope corral to catch their afternoon mounts. When the ropes start sailing around him, Smoky heads for the backside of the corral. As he is trying to figure out a way to go through, over, or under the rope cable, he spots Clint dragging a saddle over to another horse and nickers to the cowboy. Clint grins and finishes saddling his horse by the corral to be near Smoky until the remuda is turned out.

In *Smoky The Cowhorse* Will James vividly describes an open range roundup with "the wagon," consisting of three wagons pulled by teams.

The chuck wagon driven by the cook takes the lead. It is the range kitchen of the cow country, usually a farm wagon fitted at the back end with a large chuck box. The chuck box is bolted to the rear of the wagon and has a hinged lid that when let down, forms a table.

The box contains shelves and drawers to hold plates, cups, knives and forks, coffee, bacon, beans, and other food. Every chuck box has a drawer for liniment, pills, salts, and quinine, and the cook might sneak in a bottle of whiskey for personal use.

This is the domain of the uncrowned king of the big ranges, the roundup cook — also known as bean master, bisquit roller, bisquit shooter, cookie, dough-belly, dough boxer, dough puncher, dough wrangler, grub spoiler, hash burner, kitchen mechanic, lizard scorcher, mess boiler, mulligan mixer, pothooks, pot rustler, pot walloper, sizzler, sop 'n' taters, sourdough, stew builder, and swamper, among colorful others.

149

"The wagon" departing from headquarters to go o... roundup. The pilot will lead the procession followed by the chuckwagon and the woo... wagon. The "remuda" wi... be trailed along behind. (circa 1930) — Courtesy Clint and Don... Conradt, all rights reserved.

Chuckwagon from Neva... J.J. Hulton Ranch. Note chuck box bolted to rear... wagon. (circa 1915) — Nevada His... Society, Reno.

In Smoky Will James w... *"Them three wagons whi... called 'the wagon' is the cowboys' home while on... range."* (circa 1930) — Courtesy C... Donna Conradt, all rights reserved.

150

"The nighthawk in his nest." The bedroll is covered with waterproofed canvas and the cowboy can dream on regardless of the weather. L.A. Huffman photo. (circa 1915) — Montana Historical Society, Helena.

He has to be good to qualify because it is necessary for him to be both versatile and resourceful. He is the most important person in camp, and the cowboss treats him with respect. The wagon cook is aware of his aristocratic powers, and his crankiness is traditional.

He can be depended on to have three hot meals a day, rain or shine, through blistering heat or freezing cold, that are good to eat and in sufficient quantity that no matter how much company drops in there will be plenty to go around. Being mobile, his equipment is limited, yet this does not hinder his speed. On one day he may be cooking in the rain with wet wood, on another a strong wind may be scattering his fire and blowing the heat away from his pots or sand into his food. Undaunted, he may grumble but the roundup crew will be fed on time.

The bed wagon follows, driven by the flunky. It generally contains branding irons, war bags, hobbles, corral ropes, and most importantly over twenty "montana rolls."

The cowboy's bedroll is his most valued possession, and the 7x18 foot tarpaulin is made of white canvas thoroughly waterproofed. It is equipped with rings and snaps so the sleeper can pull the flap over him and fasten it. Inside are two soogans or heavy quilts, a couple of blankets, and a war bag that can be used for a pillow. In such a bed the cowboy can sleep as dry and warm as inside a house, even in

151

One of the "best in the West."
Marion Perkins (Perk) fits a
"houlihan" loop on a horse at
Arizona's Bar Cross Ranch.
— Bramlett photo.

heavy rain or snow.

The nighthawk drives the third wagon, which is used to haul wood for cooking fires on the treeless prairies. Smaller outfits use a two-wheeled cart that fastens to the rear of a chuck wagon. This cart is called a chip wagon because in the early days of the West when wood was scarce dried buffalo or cow chips were used for fuel.

The remuda, made up of over 200 head of saddle horses, comes next, driven along by the "wrangatang," the day wrangler.

James writes in *Smoky,* "Them three wagons which is called 'the wagon' is the cowboys home while on the range."

Each rider on the Rocking R, including Clint, has ten horses in his string. For some of the younger cowboys who like bucking out broncs, the cowboss cuts out extra colts for them to ride. With two or three changes of horses every day, it turns out that each horse is ridden from four to six hours every third day. That's how Smoky's turn comes around.

On large outfits the horses are roped out of the remuda. Most of the horses can't be walked up to and caught, at least not without a lot of running, and then there's the wild broncs that can't be caught any other way besides being roped. To make things simple and businesslike, all horses are caught with a *houlihan,* the horse loop.

152

There's always an exception to everything in life, and on the Rocking R outfit, Smoky is the exception. When Clint walks into that rope corral Smoky comes out of his hiding place and sticks his head into the hackamore Clint is holding. For that, Clint puts up with a lot of teasing from the other cowboys, but he does it with a big grin on his face.

Montana cowboys branding calves in the open. Will James is the second horseman from the left. Both James and distant horseman have calves roped and are waiting to drag them to the branding crew. (circa 1930)

The branding crew stamps a hot iron on a calf as "momma" cow looks on.

153

Smoky's beginning days are on outside circles, but Clint soon moves him to day-herding the steers, then he eventually graduates the willing horse to herd work. Smoky enjoys cutting out cattle that don't want to be cut and roping and dragging big fall calves to the branding fires.

Smoky is turned out on the range with the other remuda horses after the fall roundup is finished. Winter comes along with its snow and freeze-ups. The horses winter easily, and when a chinook wind starts the spring thaw Clint is the cowboy who runs the horses in. At first Smoky doesn't recognize the cowboy, until he sniffs at Clint's hand. Then he follows the grinning cowboy all around the corral.

Smoky is started on herd work during the spring roundup. He glides into a "rodear" and cuts out stock with ability and the grace of a ballet dancer, all on a slack rein. He is what a horse trainer calls a self-starter, a natural cowhorse.

There is only one thing that can be considered a discredit to the mouse-colored horse. He just has to have his little buckout every morning.

Five years pass, and Smoky becomes the top horse on the ranch. Clint is the only person to touch the animal. It makes the old cowman feel good just to watch that little horse work. His fame as a cutting horse reaches far and wide, and when it comes to roping and tripping a steer, Smoky has no peers as he reaches the height of his cowhorse career.

In those days a carload of horses could be bought for fifty dollars a head. When a letter comes to the Rocking R superintendent from a neighboring ranch offering four hundred dollars for Smoky, Clint begins to get worried. The superintendent merely laughs at that. He is proud of owning the top horse in the country. He says the only way he could sell that horse would be to fire Clint first, so he will keep him.

Will James captures Smoky's character in stories that border on the unbelievable, but horsemen know such things happen. For instance, he writes about a large steer strolling through the herd with a crooked horn that threatens to grow into its eye. When Clint

The lariat rope is the cowboy's most useful tool. Jim Bramlett "applies the twine" in rapid time. — Photo by Eva Bramlett.

spots the steer he shakes out a loop and works the critter to the outside of the herd while one of the boys spurs over to the wagon to get a saw to prune the horn. The steer breaks out of the herd, and, with its tail in the air, departs for open country.

Clint and Smoky race to the run-away. Because of the bad horn Clint ropes it around the head. Clint's rope is tied on hard and fast, and he throws his slack around the steer's hind end and turns off to trip the steer. Suddenly a loud ripping sound is heard, and Clint goes flying through the air. The tongue of the cinch tears through the worn latigo, and the saddle is pulled back on Smoky's flanks. All the boys figure it won't take a horse that can buck like Smoky very long to get rid of that saddle. There are some grins at the promise of a good show, but those grins soon change to a look of wonder at what the horse does next. When the rigging rears up, Smoky rears up with it, then wheels on those powerful hind quarters to face the steer and hold it until help arrives.

When that story is told around the campfires, many cowmen snort because they can't believe a horse is smart enough to do such a thing. But if they knew how much heart that brainy little horse has, and how willing he is to do his work, they would think differently. When he is working stock, the little horse is all business, for first, last, and always, Smoky is a cowhorse.

155

Montana range horses with long winter hair to keep them warm during the harsh winters. (circa 1930) — Courtesy Clint and Donna Conradt, all rights reserved.

Smoky is turned out with the remuda again that fall, and then winter hits with a bang. It is a rough winter with snow piling up until the fence posts around the home ranch are only an inch tall. All the cowboys, including Clint, are busy bringing in weak stock to be fed in the big sheds.

Smoky is pawing for grass with a bunch of sixteen other horses when a lone rider comes riding out of a blizzard. The horses tear out of there on a run, but the rider stays with them. Bucking the heavy drifts and wading through deep snow soon tires the horses. They finally settle down to drifting along with the storm, and always the rider follows.

This man is a halfbreed and a horsethief. He has plans for this little bunch of horses, especially Smoky, because the halfbreed has heard of the price offered for that blaze-faced grulla. The breed has his own plans to collect some money on this special horse.

The stolen horses are driven at night, and the storm covers their trail. Several months later they arrive in Arizona country. There the little bunch of horses is hazed into a corral, and the Rocking R brand is changed with a running iron to a wagon wheel. The horses are then trailed to a high mesa, where they graze until their newly changed brands heal.

Except for Clint, Smoky has a natural fear of all people. The breed tries to rope him, but the wary horse dodges. The breed becomes furious in his frustration, and when he finally catches Smoky, he ties him to a post and beats him with the limb of a tree until the horse is staggering. The rope breaks in time to save the poor horse.

156

The thief wants to break the horse's spirit. All the other stolen horses had been sold, and the breed wants to force Smoky into submission so he can sell him for a good price, but all he gets out of him is resistance. Finally, Smoky is tied to a post with no food or water, and the breed beats him mercilessly on a regular basis. Smoky eventually gives up and is ridden out and worked over with a quirt and spurs until the blood is pouring. A big hate simmers inside the horse and one day, it boils over. He "goes on the peck" and bucks the halfbreed off, then paws the man to death.

A couple of cowboys find the horse packing an empty saddle, dried blood on its jaw and legs, and murder in its eyes.

One of the cowboys likes the looks of the pony and tries to ride Smoky. He uses ropes at a distance until he throws the horse to the ground and ties its legs together. He works everything around to get a saddle on the horse, then straddles the struggling animal and takes the leg ropes off. What happens next makes the cowboy's blood run cold, and when it's over he is glad to get through the fence and safe from this savage bronc. He remembers the empty saddle and dried blood. The cowboy yells out to the horse, "A twelve-hundred-pound cougar is what you are! You damn outlaw!" That's how the mouse-colored gelding acquires the name of "The Cougar."

The outlaw fighting horse is sold to a stock contractor as a bucking bronc for rodeos and becomes a big draw. For years The Cougar's

"A bronc tossed a rider so high the birds built a nest in his hip pocket before he came back to earth." An old cowboy saying. L.A. Huffman photo. (circa 1915) — Montana Historical Society, Helena.

157

picture appears on posters for rodeos, and all who try to ride him last only two or three jumps out of the chute. They never have far to run to return to the safety of the chutes.

One day a freckled-faced cowboy comes looking for The Cougar. He is a bronc rider who has never been thrown, and he sticks longer than most riders before landing in the dust. He follows The Cougar around the country hoping to ride him, and two years later he succeeds. He is the first rodeo cowboy to ride the famous outlaw past the judge's pistol shot.

Other riders are able to ride the horse after that, and after six years as the number one bucking horse and man-fighter in the southwest, Smoky's reputation slowly fades away. His bucking continues to drop off in intensity until one day, when the chute gate is opened, he comes out on a long lope.

Old horses, like cowboys, are often misplaced individuals. Old cowboys sometimes find themselves too "stoved-up" to mount a snorting cowpony on frosty mornings, and, having to quit cowboying, become lost, drinking heavily and living in the past.

Smoky winds up in a similar lost fate. Like the cooling embers of a dying campfire, his hate for mankind diminishes and he quits bucking and fighting. When the rodeo is over, the stock is loaded and everyone pulls out, leaving a used-up, mouse-colored horse in the stock pens. Smoky had been sold to a livery stable for twenty-five dollars.

The livery man renames him Cloudy, but the name will never mean as much as when the horse was known as Smoky, the best darn cowhorse in all that northern cattle country, nor would it give people a thrill like the mere mention of The Cougar. The horse had gone from top cowhorse to champion bucking horse and now he was destined to fade away as Cloudy, a livery plug.

The old horse just gives up and goes along with whatever is asked of him. No more is there a spark in his eyes. He is being used up on his way to an early death. Everyone wants to ride the willing horse. From daylight until dark all kinds of people ride him and he becomes so tired in mind and body he barely exists.

Webster defines horse sense as being common sense. A horse can't talk; he can't tell the human who uses him when he feels bad or when he doesn't understand what the human wants him to do.

Some people expect a horse to think and react as a person would. Others expect horses to run like machines, wanting to turn them on to go and turn them off to stop.

Bill knew every horse had its own personality and that to be a good horseman a trainer must accept each horse for what it is. When Bill was having marital problems he once stated, "If I knew women like I know horses my troubles would be over."

An old-style bucking horse at the big rodeo in Prescott, Arizona. (circa 1967) — Bramlett photo.

The aged horse begins to get stiff in the shoulders and front legs. A girl rides him one day at a dead run up a mountain. She "bedrocks" the horse and, not knowing any better, leads the lathered-up old pony into a mountain stream and splashes cold water on him. This founders the horse, and he cannot be ridden anymore. The livery stable sells the sick horse to a man who buys such horses to use for chicken feed.

159

Smoky has too much heart to give up, and he is managing a living for himself on the little salt grass pasture where he is placed. The chicken feed man soon trades the old horse to a black-whiskered "feller" who hooks the gelding to a wagon and drives him home. Smoky had hit bottom for sure this time. His days are spent plowing a garden and hauling things around town, always with a whip stinging his bony old frame. The only food available is musty straw. The horse is about ready to let go of his hold on life and lie down and die.

A rodeo comes to that sunny town of Casa Grande, and many cattle buyers are there to buy Mexican cattle from across the border. Pancho Villa and the Yaquis Indians are continually raiding the Mexican rancher's herds, so the rancheros are dumping their cattle on the American market in order to salvage something for themselves.

The town is full of cattle buyers, and Clint is among them. He had bought the camp where many years before he had broke Smoky to ride. He had also bought the surrounding four thousand acres and was starting his own ranch. He came down to Arizona to buy cattle to stock the new outfit. Clint and a friend of his are sitting in a hotel lobby visiting, when a black-whiskered man drives up in a wagon. When this man is ready to go he picks up a whip and starts "playing a tune" on the back of the mouse-colored sack of bones that is hitched to his wagon.

As Clint watches, his temper begins to burn, and a bell rings inside his head as he recognizes Smoky. He runs outside, and bulldogs the black-whiskered man off the wagon, and gives the man a whipping with his own whip.

Clint buys the horse and ships him home to the north country. He keeps the old horse in a box stall all winter. With the best grass hay under his nose at all times and grain twice each day the old pony is able to put some meat on his bones and eventually some tallow; yet the horse seems to be dead inside.

Spring comes to the north country, and grass and flowers are everywhere. Clint runs in a little bunch of mares and colts and turns

Smoky loose with them. They all take off at a lope over the hill.

Clint knows Smoky will do just fine with all that feed around and the little colts for company. He has many fond memories of the times he and Smoky had together. He recalls how close they had been and hopes someday the old horse will remember him.

One morning as Clint steps out to fetch a pail of water he hears a nicker.

Will James wrote the last paragraph of the book in such a way as to say exactly what the reader is anxious to read.

> "Clint dropped his bucket in surprise at what he heard and then seen," Bill wrote. "For, standing out a ways, slick and shiny, was the old mouse-colored horse. The good care the cowboy had handed him and afterwards, the ramblings over the old home range, had done its work. The heart of Smoky had come to life again, and full size."
>
> *Smoky The Cowhorse*, Will James.
> Copyright © 1926Charles Scribner's Sons;
> copyright renewed 1961 Auguste Dufault.
> Reprinted with the permission of
> Charles Scribner's Sons.

. . .

Smoky The Cowhorse stirred everyone's imagination. Smoky's undying spirit in front of many obstacles is an inspiring story, but underneath it all is simply a good cowhorse, a range partner of a cowboy called Clint that was always willing to give his all.

Bill first titled the story *Smoky, A One Man Horse*, and the story ran in Scribner's Magazine as a four-part serial from April through July, 1926. In September the title was changed to *Smoky The Cowhorse* and the story appeared in book form. With its forty-two pencil drawings and four pen-and-ink drawings the book was an overwhelming success. The public eagerly accepted that smoke-colored gelding into their hearts, and *Smoky* drew the best review of any of Will James' books. One writer described the book as ". . . one of the truly great horse stories in our language." *The New York*

The American Library Association presented the prestigious Newbery Award to Will James in 1927 for his classic book, Smoky The Cowhorse.

Times heralded it as "The Black Beauty of the cow country."

Within a year *Smoky* was reprinted eleven times. It was published in six foreign language editions, and in 1929 became one of Scribner's Illustrated Classics featuring nine oil paintings.

Smoky brought fame of a different nature to Bill when it was chosen by the American Library Association for the annual Newbery Award as the best book of children's literature written in 1927. Now sixty years old, *Smoky*'s longevity deserves notice, for it has maintained itself in library collections without fanfare. The book has proven itself distinctive in style and conception and is respected as a contribution to American literature. In December, 1928, *Smoky* was put into a permanent library edition, and Bill delighted everyone at the National Arts Club in New York by appearing at the debut of the edition. He did drawings of horses and the range country for children who were present.

Three movies were made of this classic story. The 1934 version stars Victor Jory as Clint, with narrations from Will James himself

Movie poster of the 1945 20th Century Fox production of Smoky. —

162

to bridge time gaps in Smoky's growing-up process. Bill was disappointed when he heard the horse selected to play the part of Smoky was a black stallion named Rex. He had plainly stated that Smoky was a mouse-colored gelding, but there weren't too many mouse-colored horses around, and among them good-looking horses with Smoky's markings were unheard of. The stallion Rex was wise to cues and to working without restraints in front of the camera. Bill changed his mind and began to admire Rex for his abilities.

The 1945 movie has an especially warm and emotional scene in which Fred MacMurray, who plays Clint, leaps from the porch of a hotel and rescues an old Smoky from the whip of a trash hauler. The 1966 version stars Fess Parker as Clint. This movie strays a little from the original story but has a beautiful theme song, "Smoky, Try To Catch The Wind."

In *Lone Cowboy*, Will James writes about rambling over the country on his "ol' Smoky hoss." When the horse reaches old age, he keeps him around just for company.

One day the old horse quits the bunch he is running with and comes walking into camp where Bill is breaking broncs. The horse has a far-away look in its eyes. The old gelding lies down by a juniper tree with its head propped against it. When Bill hurries over to check on Smoky the horse seems okay. Bill squats on his heels and rolls a smoke as he talks to his "ol' pard" for awhile. The following morning when he looks out the window he is surprised to see Smoky in the same position. Bill runs over to the tree to find that Smoky has gone to sleep, never to wake again.

When Bill writes about himself in *Lone Cowboy* he describes how he went to work "swinging a wide loop" for an old cowman who had been wronged by his neighbors. This rancher had hired Bill to brand the neighboring ranchers' calves with his brand. The cowman gives Bill two young broncs as an enticement to persuade him to do this work. One of these broncs is Smoky. Bill later said he went on to ride the mouse-colored gelding from one end of the cow country to the other.

Will James wrote about Smoky in other books. The way he de-

Will James on Smoky? No, it is a retouched photograph of James on one of his good saddle horses in Washoe Valley, Nevada, dated 8-27-24. — Courtesy Clint and Donna Conradt, all rights reserved.

scribes him, the horse is the epitome of what a top horse in a cowboy's string should be in the early 1900s. Anthony Amaral wrote that Bill took great pride in bragging about the horse's bucking ability.

> "He had won bets from other cowboys who vowed they could ride the horse, which James encouraged, by claiming Smoky was a one-man horse. Apparently no one could ride Smoky unless they understood his bucking pattern. Smoky would buck with James too, and without provocation, but James knew the routine Smoky followed, and was able to stay aboard."
>
> — Anthony Amaral, Will James The Gilt Edged Cowboy
> Westernlore Press. 1967

Was Smoky a real horse? Anthony Amaral stated he was real, but in his book Tony describes the horse as a blue roan stallion. A blue roan's coat is a mixture of white and black hairs. This color pattern is a far cry from grulla, which is in the family of buckskin and dun colors.

When asked if there really was a Smoky, Alice didn't know for sure, although Bill always insisted the horse was real. Alice thought that Smoky was born on a drawing board in that little log and rock studio in Washoe Valley, Nevada.

The abilities of the horse in the book *Smoky* were everything Bill admired in a horse. Smoky could well have been derived from the

164

memory of all the good cow horses Bill had ridden. Those rare and perfect white markings on the horse, however, exactly matched the description of a legendary wild horse of the past.

When Bill had first arrived in the mustang country of eastern Nevada, the whole area was buzzing with excitement over the capture of a most handsome stallion called Blue Streak. Alice said Bill was among the crowd of onlookers when Rube Terrill, the rancher from Indian Creek who had caught the horse, rode the famous stallion into the main street of Minersville, a Nevada boomtown.

> "In one angle of sunlight his color was an intensified Grullo (crane-colored), indicating his Spanish ancestry; in another angle, blue black, with sheen of grackle, except for white stockings and blazed face. His small hoofs were flint hard. All his flesh seemed to be deer-leg muscles, integrated by the finest steel springs. His neck had the curve of the bronze horses of Lysippus, which stood on Nero's arch in Rome and now animate the front of St. Mark's Cathedral in Venice. His back was saddle perfect.

> "Give you $500 for him," someone yelled. Excited by the sight of so many people, Blue Streak pranced on even more magnificently as his owner yelled back, "$750 wouldn't touch him.

> Temple yelled again, "I guess a $1,000 would."

> — J. Frank Dobie, *The Mustangs*,
> Curtis Publishing Co., 1934

The horse was sold to Abner Temple, a mining magnate from Utah. Temple shipped the horse home to Salt Lake City, where he rode the strinkingly handsome horse around town and in parades.

One night the stallion kicked down a wall of his stall. He crossed the Great Salt Plains and returned to his range in Nevada. Temple hired a crew to capture the runaway.

The men eventually cornered the stallion, along with four mares, on the edge of a lofty escarpment. The proud stallion paused briefly and then, followed by his remaining harem, he chose death over relinquishing his freedom a second time and leaped over the edge onto the rocks below.

The bone-chilling spectacle remained forever in the minds and hearts of the onlooking mustangers. Blue Streak's story was told countless times in cow camps and mustanger camps all over the West.

The young Will James had idolized this wild stallion, and when he wrote and illustrated *Smoky* he used the same, exact color and markings of Blue Streak.

> *Sentinels of alertness in eye and nostril*
> *Every toss of maned neck a Grecian grace,*
> *Every high snort bugling out the pride of the free.*
>
> — J. Frank Dobie, *The Mustangs*,
> Curtis Publishing Company, 1934

— Courtesy Bureau of Land Management.

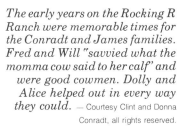
The early years on the Rocking R Ranch were memorable times for the Conradt and James families. Fred and Will "savvied what the momma cow said to her calf" and were good cowmen. Dolly and Alice helped out in every way they could.

Chapter VI

"A COW OUTFIT OF MY OWN"

"There's something about having a good hunk of land that makes big money seem like nothing but a lot of trouble. But I have to have some money to square up on that hunk I have and square up on all my obligations. After that I sure plan on living on my land and from my cattle. I'll want to draw and write and paint of course but that will be like for pleasure and I'm thinking I'll do better work then. Mixing my writing with riding is my idea of fine and peaceful living, and reaching on for big and bigger money won't get no grey hairs in my head."

— Letter from Will James to Burt Twitchell, 1934.

167

"THE CROW COUNTRY is good a country," Chief Arapooish once said. "It has plenty of water for my people and their ponies. Its mountain forests provide poles for our lodges. Its plains are covered with grass for many buffaloes. The Crow country is a good country."

When someone has ridden into such a country, with its white-capped peaks, forested ridges where the wapiti lives, foothills sloping down to grassy plains that stretch farther than the eye can see; and when he has drunk from the sparkling, magic water of the high country, he will always want to return.

Will James drank from these waters. He chased mustangs over the dry foothills. He cut his teeth on cattle roundups to the north, where he matured as a cowboy. Like Arapooish, he felt this was his country, and he loved it.

Bill closed his eyes and puffed earnestly on a freshly lit Bull Durham cigarette. His mind's eye could see a green valley with a stream meandering through the center of it. Rugged, red bluffs rimmed along both sides of the valley, building in a high crescendo of vibrating colors to a brilliant red peak. A proud, black stallion approached a pinnacle to survey the country below. He stood with thin nostrils extended, testing the air, ears forward, projecting their senses for even the slightest of sounds. The veins protruded on his head, and his eyes bulged as a strong breeze riffled through his mane and tail.

Suddenly he wheeled on muscular hindquarters, and in less than a heartbeat he vanished from all senses of sight and sound. But the vision of his wild presence remained forever in the mind and the hungry side of a wanderer's heart.

The wild country beckoned as a breeze whispered through the sagebrush and built to a loud chorus among the cathedrals of towering ponderosa pines. A man listened and understood, for it was a wanderer's song, his song.

Will James pushed back from his drawing board, the same drawing board where he created a special, smoke-colored horse. He blew out the lamp and strolled outside into the moonlit night.

Bill felt restless. He lit another cigarette and leaned on the corral fence. Horses in the corral snorted and paced to the far end, where they wheeled and stood with their heads held high to watch each move the man made.

Bill sniffed the Nevada air and rolled another twirly. His thoughts were far away, recalling images of a long time ago when he had ridden a jaded horse into a sheltered valley rimmed by red sandstone bluffs. While trying in vain to turn a herd of mustangs toward a distant trap, he had used his horse to its limits. He'd stripped his rigging from the lathered horse's back to give the pony a chance to cool down and regain its wind, then had lain back in the green grass and rolled a smoke. The ground smelled good, meadowlarks were singing, and flowers were everywhere. If he ever decided to settle down, he'd thought, this little paradise would do just fine. He would build a round breaking corral on the open ground and a few horse corrals behind it. The house would fit nicely in that bend of the river.

Out of the corner of his eye Bill noticed a slight movement on a

169

bluff, and for a split second time had stood still. It was then he had caught the fleeting glimpse of the horse he would never be able to forget in his lifetime, the black stallion.

As Bill stood by the corral in that Nevada night he wondered how many times he had recalled the mental picture of that black stud horse.

He strolled into the log house where Alice lay asleep on a divan in front of the fireplace. Reflections from the flickering fire danced across her face and highlighted her fair blond hair. Bill felt a pang as he looked at the familiar face. If only he could tell her that he felt incomplete when he was closed in, when things became too staid, how a restlessness beyond his control chewed at his insides until he reached the point of having no peace of mind. If only he had the words to help her understand he needed some freedom to be creative, to be his own man, to make his own decisions; tonight he had made a big one.

Morning came, and as the sun peaked over the desert hills it bathed the whole of Washoe Valley in a golden light. With breakfast over, Alice and Bill stepped outside and walked along to the horse corrals. Bill was in a silent mood, and Alice sensed there was something building in him and that they were on the verge of a confrontation. Her thoughts were interrupted by an unexpected visitor.

Will and Alice on two good horses. (circa 1932) — Courtesy Les Pons.

"Oh, no!" she muttered under her breath. "Here comes ol' what's-his-name."

A neighbor of the Jameses came storming up to them. He took a stand with his hands on his hips. The retired man's gray hair fairly bristled with his anger. "James," he yelled, "you must do something about this horse manure. The wind blows the stench through the windows and right into my house, and just look at all those flies!"

Bill calmly rolled a Bull Durham cigarette, licked the edge to glue it shut, then twirled the end before putting it in his mouth. He struck a match and lit up, took a deep puff, and looked out across the valley, "Guess you won't have to worry about my hosses no more," he drawled.

"I. . .I won't?".

"No siree," Bill retorted. "Except to be movin' 'fore long. I'm planning to sell out to a pig farmer."

"A PIG FARMER!" the neighbor screamed. "Oh, my God, I'll buy this place from you and pay more than any pig farmer."

Bill chuckled, but Alice stood in shocked surprise until the old gentleman had left. The pattern of life in Washoe Valley had become comfortable and predictable for her, and she did not want to give up her security. However, Bill was her man, and she would go to the end of the world with him if need be.

"This valley's gettin' too crowded for me," Bill explained, while avoiding her eyes. "I need to be where I can throw a rope without gettin' it caught on a fence post."

"What do you mean?" Alice asked, alarmed.

"I mean," Bill answered, "that I need to head out to the tall and uncut."

"Where is that?" Alice demanded, dreading the answer.

"To Montana, my birth state," he explained to her. "I plan to start us a ranch!"

What was talk one day became a reality the next, and things moved rapidly after that. The Nevada property was sold, and Alice

Dolly Conradt sits a big, gray horse on Will James' Rocking R Ranch located in the Crow Indian country of southern Montana (circa 1930) — Courtesy Clint and Donna Conradt, all rights reserved.

Dolly's riding gloves, made on the Crow Indian reservation. (circa 1930) — Courtesy Clint and Donna Conradt, all rights reserved.

172

and Dolly began packing. Fred was hired as foreman of the ranch-to-be, and the two friends, Bill and Fred, headed for southern Montana and the Crow Indian reservation to make Bill's dream ranch, the Rocking R, a reality.

The Crow country lay in a southerly direction from Billings and Pryor, Montana. The reservation was about the size of the state of New Jersey. A sparsely inhabited area, it was the country Bill had dreamed of for many years. Bands of mustangs could be seen on the ridges and badlands that rolled back to the Pryor and Big Horn mountains. Buffalo skulls could be found here and there. Arrowheads could be picked up by the handful, reminiscent of buffalo-hunting days and battles between the Crows and their ancestral enemies, the Sioux. A few miles away, at Crow Agency, was Custer's battlefield.

> There is a trader's store at the subagency of Pryor, Montana, on the Crow reservation, which is the business and social center of a vast free space peopled mostly by Indians, cowboys and freighters.
>
> Crow Indians gather at the store, as they have been doing for many years. One gets the pad-pad of moccasined feet on the floor. Bargains are driven with an astounding economy of speech between traders and customers. After their brief barter is over the Indians lean back against the counters. The men wear store clothes and affect a peculiarly high crowned felt hat, which is held in place by a band under the chin. Their hair supplies the one barbaric touch, being done in twin braids. The women wear calico dresses of their own make, with bright

Crow Indians heading for the trader's store at the Pryor Subagency. (circa 1927) — Montana Historical Society, Helena.

173

shawls to cover their heads. And the average white girl is no more meticulous in the application of lipstick than the Indian girl is in seeing that there is a streak of vermilion along the part of her glossy black hair.

If reservation gossip is exchanged, apparently it is carried on in sign language, as few words are spoken. One gets the impression of being in a lazy, comfortable backwash, remote from the general current of things, where he talks little, rolls many cigarettes and gets bravely over the idea that time is of any particular importance.

The Billings Gazette, February 9, 1930

There was always a ripple of interest when a newcomer arrived, so all eyes were turned to the road as a cloud of dust rapidly approached the trading post. The car braked to a stop, and the cloud of dust caught up to and engulfed it. Out of the dust stepped two big-hatted Nevada cowboys, Will James and Fred Conradt.

They made their way into the store, where they engaged the trader in conversation to gain information on certain kinds of land.

Bill knew that old Arapooish's praise of the Crow country still held good; the buffalo were all gone, but at the time this was cattle country. Instead of buying a ready-made ranch, he was determined to build one up from the raw prairie. To that end he bought enough of what is known as 'dead Indian land' to give himself some elbow room. Dead Indian land was property that was subject to sale because no heirs had claimed it after the death of the Indian owner.

Bill's piecing together of parcels of land proved to be brilliant. Over a period of the next several years he bought and leased a total of 8,000 acres. He chose for ranch headquarters that part of the valley that had occupied a special place in his heart for so many years. He would often saddle up and ride to the top of a nearby red pinnacle where he had caught a glimpse of that wild, black stallion so long ago.

Bill stocked the ranch with Angus and horned Hereford cattle,

Will James imported a herd of multi-colored longhorn cattle to his ranch in Montana. He was concerned that the historic breed of cattle would become extinct.

— Bramlett photo.

and Fred decided to ship in a few Charolais bulls to put added weight on fall calves. Replacement heifers from these crosses proved to be hardy cattle in Montana winters. There were no perimeter fences or close neighbors, and the stock ranged far and wide.

"I want to keep alive what is passing in the West," Bill publicly stated, and he meant it. He backed up his words with action by buying and importing a small herd of the nearly extinct Texas Longhorn cattle from the Wichita Mountains Wildlife Refuge in Oklahoma. They found that crossing Longhorn bulls with first calf heifers of the English breeds gave them practically trouble-free calving because of the small size of the Longhorn calves.

Bill loved those longhorns. He enjoyed giving friends and guests a rundown on the multi-colored cattle with their big "antlers." He told about the trail drives from Texas and how these rangy cattle fed the nation after the Civil War. He compared the longhorn with the old-time cowman, both of which he said were tough and high-headed.

The Rocking R Ranch was open and Western. Elk and deer appeared in large herds in late winter, and big cat tracks could be seen below the canyon rims. The cattle were worked in the manner of the old-time outfits, with style and efficiency. When a cow needed to be doctored she wasn't driven to corrals miles away. Instead she was

175

roped, tied down, and doctored on the spot. The Rocking R ran a wagon during the spring and fall roundups. The daily gathers were held right out in the open, where Dolly and the cowboys roped out calves and snaked them over to a branding fire. As soon as a calf was branded it went right back to its mammy. Bill had a nice little outfit put together, and he and Fred knew how to run the cow end of it and how to handle their livestock.

"We had more horses than we needed," Dolly said in remembering those early days, "but Bill liked his horses. If he seen one that struck his fancy, he bought it. He had a special fondness for the big draft horses. One day when I was milking the cow I heard Bill talking to a team of Percheron work horses under a lean-to. 'Old-timers,' he said, 'they're taking away all that's good in the West, you too.'"

Those first few years on the Rocking R Ranch were idyllic times for both the James and the Conradt families, as they all worked together. Dolly was a good hand on a horse and was invaluable help to Fred when sorting, moving, and doctoring cattle.

"I think you better get a cook," Bill wrote to Fred from Hollywood in 1934. "I'd rather see Dolly riding than sticking around a stove and you washing dishes after you're tired out from a day's work. I don't think I could stand Dolly's cooking anyhow, and besides, there'll be some more haying to do and then branding and shipping. You ought to be able to get a pretty good cook now, get the 'motherly' kind."

At a time when many women lived in their housecoats, the petite Dolly changed directly into her Western riding skirt when she came

Will James' favorites, a team of Percheron work horses. (circa 1932) —

(a)Alice and Will James give baby Clint his first horseback ride. (circa 1928) — Courtesy Clint and Donna Conradt, all rights reserved.

(b)In 1931 Bill wrote a book about his favorite nephew, Clint. Bill never failed to send the lad a present from New York when business called him there. Usually it was a toy, but this time it was a newspaper clipping describing a book that a lonesome man had written about a little cowboy. — Courtesy Clint and Donna Conradt, all rights reserved.

(c)A Will James sketch showing Clint obsessed with the roping fever. — Courtesy Clint and Donna Conradt, all rights reserved.

(d)A pint-sized Clint wants to show his uncle Bill that he is "big-enough" to be a cowboy. — Courtesy Clint and Donna Conradt, all rights reserved.

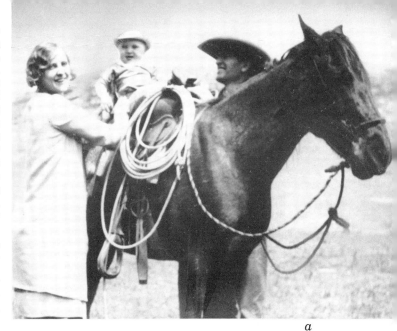

a

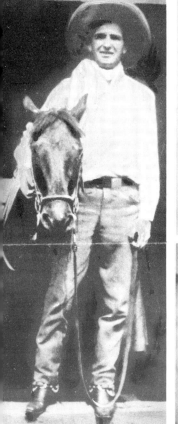

b

c

d

177

a

b

*(d)*Big - Enough, *by Will James,
published in 1931.*

c

d

178

Dolly Conradt drives an old buck rake.

back from the hospital with her new son. When Clint was born, it was a time for celebration on the ranch. Fred was a gentle husband and father, and Bill had the honor of naming his nephew. He chose the name Clint after the leading character in *Smoky The Cow Horse*.

Clint's Uncle Bill doted on the child. When Bill was on business trips, Clint was the recipient of many unique toys. There was a steady string of letters and cards sent to the youngster, and he was always mentioned in Bill's letters to Fred and Dolly. "And how is old-timer Clint?" Bill wrote at the end of a letter in 1934. "I hope you still like your carrots. I seen a little boy with a little car just like yours pass all the big cars on the street the other day, but the other cars was all standing still."

Donna Conradt tells with delight how Bill, when Clint was a boy, bought a little pony complete with saddle and bridle and hauled the pony home to Clint in the back seat of his convertible. In 1931 Bill dedicated his book *Big Enough* to Clint.

Fred Conradt rescues an unfortunate traveler on the road to the Rocking R Ranch. —

179

The ranch house at the Rocking R Ranch south of Billings, Montana. Will James' studio is to the right. (circa 1930) —

The studio and cook house. Guests ate at the same table with the ranch hands. The canvas flap at the end of the cook house rolled up to ventilate the room. (circa 1930) —

Will James and visitor on the front porch of the ranch house. Note deer and elk horns on roof and buffalo skull at the men's feet. (circa 1930) —

180

Inside the James ranch house.

Mementos of the old West were placed around the grounds of the ranch house. Alice and Will James pose with a large buffalo skull.

An authentic Crow Indian teepee was set up at the rear of the ranch house for guests.

181

There were many cattle on the Pryor ranch, so a large quantity of hay was cut and put up for winter feeding. The ranch was a busy place, but it was managed in an orderly fashion and consequently there was always time for entertaining guests.

Bill's ranch was remote, and he planned to keep it that way. He would not permit the 45 miles of dirt road from Pryor to be paved. The washboard road was a standard joke in Billings, where they called it the James Kidney Rocker.

"You know, I like my section of the country because it has poor roads," Bill said with his usual grin. "If the roads were fixed up, tourists would be swarming all over the place."

Visiting celebrities, movie stars, publishers, and other dignitaries were often guests at the picturesque ranch. Once the road was behind them their stay became enjoyable.

"We had the most wonderful meals," one guest said in describing her visit, "and having to walk a trail to get to the cook house helped our appetites. There was a Chinese cook and all the 'hands' ate at this central cook house. One end of it was open completely to the outdoors."

When approaching the ranch house, a summer visitor was aware of the buzzing of locusts in the poplars and willows surrounding the building. A tall, authentic Indian teepee was set up in the rear for adventurous guests and mementos of the Old West were lying around the grounds, much to the delight of everyone.

The house was not too large. It had a bedroom in one end, a large living room with a stone fireplace in the center, Indian rugs, leather furnishings, and pictures and animal horns on the walls. Bill's studio was to one side, and was very low, as was the building itself. One could look out a window and see a trail going downhill to the "library" among the willows.

The initial arguments between Bill and Alice began over this "library" outhouse. Bill wanted to keep alive a frontier-like tradition on the Rocking R, and he refused to allow an inside bathroom. Alice was humiliated and told him an outhouse was too old-fashioned. Bill persisted and delighted in observing the dismay of

182

Alice and Dolly in town clothes and ready for a trip to Billings, Montana, for some shopping and a bath. Will James had a room at the Grand hotel permanently reserved in his name. (circa 1930) —

his eastern guests when they inquired about the facilities. Bill pointed toward the path. He also pointed out the creek and where they could bathe.

Alice reluctantly gave in and painted the outhouse so it was cheerful and bright. After cleaning her brushes she tossed the rags, soaked with solvent, down the hole. Later Bill went into the outhouse with his inevitable cigarette, which he threw down the hole. Alice heard a loud BOOM! and rushed from the house in time to see Bill staggering out of the little building. As he pulled up his pants Alice saw that his face and other parts of his body were blackened with ashes. Visibly scared, Bill looked at Alice and back at the outhouse, where smoke was boiling out of the half moon cut into the door.

"My God!" he exclaimed, "the damn thing blew up!"

For those who didn't feel too Western, Bill had a room at the Grand Hotel in Billings permanently reserved in his name. Alice and Dolly made good use of this room for baths during shopping trips.

The Jameses and the Conradts delighted in taking guests on overnight horseback rides. When the lucky visitors returned to their homes they took with them the memory of a truly Western experience in the Pryor hills.

In 1966, a former resident of the Clarks Fork Valley (a fertile farming area which lies to the west of Pryor) described her first encounter with the famous artist/writer from the Pryor hills.

183

"One day a low, long, black convertible with red leather upholstery cut out roaring and dust raised high in the air on our dirt road, came right to our acre corner and made a turn down a neighborhood lane," she said. "The chickens squawked and ran for their lives, our dog barked like crazy, and we ran for the fence to get a closer look at all the noise! It was Will James, he was visiting our neighbor down the lane. He shouted, waved and smiled at us and was very friendly as he raced by.

"When Mrs. James and Will came to Billings they were conspicuous on the street as they were both handsome people," she went on to say. "Even if you did not recognize Mr. James, he had every appearance of a celebrity. He wore beautiful hats and boots. He was always immaculate in a white shirt, and with a black bow tie most of the time. His coloring was absolutely natural but he looked 'made up' as he was so tanned and his high cheek bones were always ruddy. The contrast of this coloring with his dark brown eyes and very dark hair was attractive and clean cut. He was tall and lean. He looked best with his hat on, maybe because his haircut was a brunet version of a Mark Twain haircut, however, short and less bouffant. He always wore sleeveholders which kept his cuffs pulled up past his wrists, showing his gifted hands. The cowboys in his art had his posture, the lean figure, and even his haircut in the back of his head, but his cowboys were not handsome of face like he was and I always wondered why. Will James could have acted in movies and been as colorful as Bill Hart or Tom Mix ever were, I believe."

Will James with Dolly on one side and Alice on the other posing with guests outside James' studio. (circa 1930) —

184

Bill later engaged this young lady to type the manuscript for a recently completed novel. The girl bought some riding "duds", and with a girlfriend for company drove out to the ranch. The next morning she was ready to go to work.

"I had brought my own typewriter," she later wrote, "and Will James gave me the manuscript of *Sand*, a few instructions, and then left. This was the most beautiful handwritten manuscript, so orderly, even the interlined additions and corrections. Everything was so neat, just like the house, just like the Jameses. As I converted his handsome writing into routine typewritten pages I felt something was abandoned or had become barren about the story. I was so intrigued by that sheaf of pages all completely full and perfect, as if he did it at one sitting, reread and added corrections at the second sitting and that was it. I have wondered since, what happened to that lovely handwritten manuscript as it too, was a work of art and had as much character as his horses. The loops of the letters were as perfect as the muscles and tendons of Smoky.

"I cannot remember too much about the work involved in typing the book, as these people were so gracious to us that a holiday or vacation for us seemed to be more important. Every evening we rode horses and when the sun had set we would talk and sing cowboy songs in the living room until bedtime.

"I do remember the first day's typing when I was alone and struggling to correct his grammar as I typed. When he came to look at what I had done he did not scold me, but laughed and laughed, wondering 'How in the hell his book would sell with cowboys speaking correct English.'"

City visitors pose with Fred Conradt at a picnic on the Rocking R Ranch. (circa 1932)

185

Many people left the Rocking R Ranch with glowing accounts of their visits, but those days were rapidly coming to an end. Ominous dark clouds were appearing on the horizon, and a feeling of change was in the wind, a change that would ultimately affect all the folks on the Rocking R. Bill began to drink heavily.

Bill was a self-made man and a simple cowboy at heart, all cowboy. When working on ranches he had fallen into the same pattern of most other hands. He would work hard for his money, often twelve- or fifteen-hour workdays in both sunshine and bad weather. When paid, he headed for town with his pards and went out drinking and partying. The spree ended when all his money was spent, and then he returned to work.

This same pattern presented itself on the Rocking R. Upon completion of a book or story, Bill would announce to Alice that he had "a new one packed up, lashed down with a diamond, and sent on its way." Then he headed for town and went on a bender. Some of these drinking spells lasted three or four days.

With many visiting celebrities on the ranch, evening parties were commonplace. Bill was caught up in the growing aura of Will James the celebrity, and in those early years the recognition of his adoring public suited him just fine. But life was becoming too complicated for a simple cowboy, and he became easy prey to compulsive drinking. Frequent invitations to ride in parades and to appear at rodeos in Billings, Helena, or Missoula often ended at a party, and Bill couldn't resist having one more drink.

A horse is judged by how much heart it has. Bill must have had a lot of heart to come back from those drinking spells and produce work as he did. But the man had his dream to pay for, an eight-thousand acre ranch.

In October, 1928, Bill and Alice went to New York. Bill starred in a rodeo at Madison Square Garden. He introduced each event and presented trophies to the grinning cowboys. He also had an exhibit of his drawings in the lobby along with copies of his books, which eager readers purchased to have him autograph. Afterwards, Bill headed for the chutes to visit with the cowboys.

Later that day a note was delivered to Alice which read, "Gone with the boys for a spell." Bill was carried back that night, dead drunk.

"He never seemed to know what he was doing when he drank," Tony Amaral wrote. "When in such a state James was uninhibited. The turn of a thought in his mind was quickly enacted. Once in New York, he led the rodeo parade. Suddenly, he reined his horse off the street, rode into a prominent hotel, and shot at the lobby lights. Texas, Hollywood and Montana also would be branded with James' wild cowboy capers."

In the city of Billings, Montana there is a school named Will James Junior High School. The city has a fountain that is also named after Will James, thanks to Mayor Willard E. Fraser.

"Genius should never be judged by normal human standards, and as for me, I accept genius where I find it," began Willard E. Fraser in 1967, "and Will James was a genius, and he was great, and he was ours, and the Mayor of Billings is his partisan.

"Shortly after I became Mayor the county commissioners were going to tear down the fountain on our courthouse lawn that, for years, had been known as 'the fountain of no names.' The youth of Billings were tempted to mix detergents and other foreign substances into the fountain with great glee, especially when the paper carried stories reporting same.

187

"I moved into the picture and in a fit of pique, the county commissioners said if the mayor thinks he is so smart, he can have the damn fountain. I quickly accepted it. Later the press were in my office wondering what I was going to do with the fountain, now that I owned it. I said we are going to make it run, but first of all we have changed the name from 'the fountain of no names' to The Will James Fountain. The press reporters being generally newcomers to Billings wanted to know why. I explained that Will was probably the only Billings resident in my lifetime who would be read and thought about in the next hundred - five hundred years from now, for he wrote one of the finest animal stories [*Smoky*] ever written, and for that reason I thought it was time Billings began to take cognizance of him.

"The next day an elderly lady came rushing into my office and exclaimed, 'Why in the world did you name the fountain Will James, Mayor?' I gave her the above reasons and she replied, 'Yes, but a *water* fountain after Will James, why Mayor, he didn't know what water was.'"

Letter to Anthony Amaral from
Mayor Willard E. Fraser, Billings, 1967

On a high pinnacle.
— Bramlett photo.

Chapter VII

THE BLACK STALLION

*"Running mustangs has got to be an old game for me. It'd got so
that instead of getting pleasure and excitement out of seeing a
wild bunch running smooth into our trap corrals I was finding
myself wishing they'd break through the wings and get away."*

Sun Up, Will James
Copyright © 1931 Charles Scribner's Sons;
copyright renewed 1961 Auguste Dufault.
Reprinted with the permission of
Charles Scribner's Sons.

THE BLACK STALLION approached the rim with caution. He was a lone horse because he had quit his band of mares when pursued by some mustangers. His run for freedom had taken the proud horse across miles of prairie country and over a low range of mountains. The stud horse was leg weary, but a bright fire burned in his eyes. He had a small head on a slim neck, long sloping hips, and muscles that rippled under a shiny, black hide. As the handsome horse surveyed the valley he created a picture no horseman could soon forget.

The stallion spotted a horse among the willows in the valley below. The stud was lonesome for his own kind. He wheeled around and began to pick his way down the bluff.

The sound of approaching hoofbeats caused Bill's saddle horse to raise its head. As Bill lay in the grass and watched the wild, free spirit of a horse on the pinnacle he scarcely breathed for fear of spooking it. And now he could hear the stallion coming toward him at a dead run.

The black broke over a small hill and raced into view with nostrils flared wide, showing red as they sucked in air. The horse skimmed across the valley floor and bore down upon the man. The stallion raced ever nearer until finally it was close enough for Bill to see its eyes, where fear showed plainly.

Suddenly Bill was aware of a rider behind the worn-out stud. The man had a rope in his hands, and he shook out a loop. Whirling it a couple of times, he projected the loop over the speeding black.

"No!" Bill screamed, "No! No!"

Alice put her hand on Bill's arm. "It's alright, honey," she said in a soothing voice. "You were dreaming."

Bill blinked his eyes and stared around the hospital room. It was white. The walls were white, the curtains and sheets were white, and the vision of the black horse faded rapidly from his mind.

"The doctor said it's a good thing we rushed you to the hospital," Alice went on to say. "You almost didn't make it. He had to operate on you for appendicitis." Bill felt weak. He drifted back to sleep.

190

In 1928 Will and Alice James traveled to New York City for a series of lectures and autograph parties. —

During the next several days Bill simply existed. He would not eat because food didn't smell good to him. All he wanted was a drink. He was getting weaker and weaker. Alice finally told him that he reminded her of a sheep the way he gave up and that maybe he should consider changing his profession and become a sheepherder. That statement got an instant reaction from Bill.

"Don't call me a damn sheepherder!" he yelled.

Bill was mad all over, but he woke up and began to fight back. He ate his dinner that evening, and the next day his complexion didn't resemble the color of hospital sheets anymore.

The appendicitis operation took place in a Reno hospital in 1927, but the dream of the black stallion haunted Bill for years.

Upon Bill's release from the hospital the Jameses returned to their new ranch in Montana. Once in the country Bill regained his strength remarkably fast and became his old self, the easy-going cowboy people liked so well.

In the summer of 1928 Alice and Bill boarded a train to New York City for a conference with Bill's publisher, Charles Scribner's Sons. Arriving in town, they were pleased to discover the publishing house had scheduled an itinerary throughout the metropolitan area for Bill to lecture and autograph books.

The couple rented an apartment on Madison Avenue and went right to work. Bill's conferences lasted several days with Scribner's editor, Maxwell Perkins, and also with Whitney Darrow, the vice

191

UNCLE BILL

A TALE OF TWO KIDS
AND A COWBOY

By
WILL JAMES

Uncle Bill, *by Will James,
published in 1932.*

president who managed Bill's business interest with the firm. Mr. Darrow agreed to his author's request for a sizeable advance against the royalties of his next book to offset operating expenses at the ranch.

New York's overwhelming response to Bill's talks and book-signing parties caught the Jameses by surprise. Fans swarmed to the sessions to see this bowlegged cowboy and to hear him talk in his cowboy jargon about the West.

At first Bill enjoyed all the attention he received at such well-known places as Macy's bookstores. He was touched by the sincerity of children who came to see the man who had written *Smoky*. Bill always obliged them when they asked him to draw a horse or tell a story. He told Alice, "Someday I'm gonna write a story just for kids who want to come west. I know how they feel." He did write three books for children: *Uncle Bill*, 1932, *In The Saddle With Uncle Bill*, 1935, and *Look See With Uncle Bill*, 1938.

The Jameses were overly busy. Evenings were never their own, as they were obliged to attend social affairs given in Bill's honor by magazine publishers and literary and library associations. Bill began to tire of the city and the people who lived there.

In all metropolitan areas life was too complicated for him, causing him to become restless and irritable. He dreamed of simple daily routines, of riding through his cattle as meadowlarks sang in the grass. He could close his eyes and picture herds of mustangs grazing in a desert basin. He often thought of a wild, black stallion running

192

free across a limitless space of silence, the only sound that of hooves striking soft dirt.

Bill bitterly resented cities. They reminded him of the year he had spent in prison. Behind those prison walls people had been around him constantly. He couldn't get away from them. The closeness had been stifling, and it became hard for him to breathe. Sometimes when he drank enough he could drive those feelings away and feel free again.

There were two things Bill desired in life, and one of them was to live on his own ranch. He wanted to have a corral full of good cow horses and to be able to ride out across the desert in a classical land of space and silence. He not only wanted to return permanently to the range country, but he also wanted to improve his oil painting. Deep inside he felt he could paint as well as Charlie Russell if he could only find time to work at it.

Bill was caught between two worlds. He was unable to live the life for which he yearned on the Rocking R, and he spent an increasing

193

In 1933 Will James went to Hollywood,
where he made appearances in Fox
Studios' Smoky The Cowhorse. —

majority of his time in the concrete canyons of those cities he
disliked so much. He had to pay for his ranch, and he was beginning
to worry that he had bitten off more than he could chew.

Both Scribner's and Alice wanted Bill to tour upstate New York
with his lectures, but the cowboy'd had enough. He told them he was
heading back to the "wide open spaces." At this stage of his life,
drinking had become a daily habit, and alcohol did not agree with
him. He would frequently undergo complete personality changes
when drunk. After the couple returned to the ranch, Alice wrote her
mother saying she would leave Bill if he did not quit his excessive
drinking.

In the summer of 1933, Bill went to Hollywood. He had sold the
movie rights for *Smoky The Cow Horse* to Fox Studios. They also
hired Bill to make appearances in the film. The script writers had
written narration scenes for Bill, which showed him at his drawing
board. His job was to narrate the horse's growing-up process in the
sequences where Smoky matured from foal to yearling to full grown.

Bill visited the Jones stable where, years before, he had been a
stuntman and rider for silent Westerns. The purpose of his visit to

194

Edendale was to see Rex, the black stallion selected to play the part of his "ol' Smoky hoss."

Rex was a proud, handsome animal, and director Eugene Forde considered him a natural for the part because the horse had such presence. The sensitive animal was dangerous, however, and would fight with little provocation.

The stallion was teased to provoke his anger for the filming of the scenes in which "Smoky fought the feeling of a strange hand." The horse became vicious and pursued two of the cowboys. The results were scary, and in the final edit of the film Forde had to cut the scene. It was too real, and he feared irate response from the public.

Seeing the fierce horse stirred memories in Bill. That night in his hotel room, with a bottle for company, he thought back to the days of his youth in eastern Canada, when he had daydreamed of capturing a wild, black stallion all for himself and riding the powerful steed across the Western landscape as free as the wind.

Sadly out of control, Bill was caught up in a social whirl in Hollywood. Not only were studios filming a movie of *Smoky*, they were also filming his autobiography, *Lone Cowboy*. The cowboy hero was invited to actors' ranch estates in the San Fernando valley and to producers' homes in Palm Springs for nightly cocktail parties. Bill made them all and reached the point of no return in his headlong dash toward alcoholism.

Bill hated living in the city for such prolonged periods. In an alcoholic state he would dream of younger, carefree days when his will was the "will of the wind" and he had roamed the sagebrush flats and the red, eroded hills of the country he loved. He would be mounted on a smoke-colored saddle horse, and all his possessions would be in a bedroll that was lashed to a packhorse. His only responsibility had been to find a good spot to camp where he could hobble his ponies on tall feed and cook himself a "bait." Always, before he drifted off to sleep, he would think back to the day he had seen that black stallion silhouetted against the Montana sky on a high, red pinnacle. Its long mane and tail whipping in the wind, the stallion was completely free to go where it wanted when it wanted.

This stallion was an integral part of Bill's make-up, a symbol of freedom, a freedom he knew would never again be his.

. . .

Autographed Smoky *Classic Edition.*

Will James wrote twenty-four books about cowboying and chasing mustangs. Throughout his books the black stallion pops up regularly. In his first novel, *Smoky The Cow Horse*, published in 1926, a black range stud whips the three-year-old Smoky and sends him on his way. In Bill's short story from *Sun Up*, entitled "Midnight" and again in "The Last Catch" from the same book, the leading characters each capture a handsome, wild, and intelligent black stallion. In both accounts, Bill turns the horses loose because his conscience won't let him keep such a free spirit in captivity. There is a poetic inspiration in his writing about this mustang that he always leaves running loose on the desert. Bill seemed to have a need within himself to know that that black stallion was out there in the rugged, sage-covered wastelands, as free as the wind. The

196

reader is left with the abstract impression that this wild horse could be found, and perhaps even caught if one had the knowledge and the guts.

Sand, published in 1929, is Bill's ultimate black stallion story. In an essay written in 1985, Jane Nelson has some interesting comments about this book:

> Upon the novel's publication, James received mixed reviews from his readers for the first time. Perhaps responding to the quality of caricature in the first few chapters, F. Van der Water of the New York Evening Post grumbled about James' 'perversity in spelling' and 'smug belief that all virtue is sequestered between the Missouri and the Rockies.' Yet, as his first novel featuring human characters with human emotions — love, jealousy, regret and pride — *Sand* contains some very interesting fictional elements and remains one of the best novels in the entire cannon of James' work.
>
> *—Will James: The Spirit of the Cowboy,*
> Nicolaysen Art Museum, Casper, Wyoming, 1985.

In the opinion of many buckaroos, the most exciting and inspiring example of Bill's writing is in the chase and capture of a magnificent stallion in *Sand*. It is an adventure of legendary proportions, believable to both novice and expert mustangers.

As in all successful hunts, the chase begins with a necessary ingredient, luck. Tilden, the main character in the book, has spent several years in hot pursuit of this horse. In the "school of hard knocks" he has learned all he could about cowboying and the psychology of horses.

Tilden builds a hidden trap on a high, juniper-covered ridge that leads to a pass in the mountains beyond. In his pursuits, he had noted that this was one of the black's favorite escape routes. His attempts to catch the horse had failed the previous year, so the next spring he heads back with a supply-laden pack horse in tow, ready to resume the hunt.

Tilden is riding through a stand of junipers when he notices some

197

horses that look like the black stallion's band of mares. He is about to ride by when one of the horses catches his attention. He pulls up to stare.

That one animal, which before had been feeding, had of a sudden raised a head, sniffed the air, and then begin to circle around the bunch like as if worried about something. Tilden noticed the jet-black and shiny hide of that horse, the long flowing mane and tail, and, as he started the bunch to move, Tilden stared on, unbelieving. But there was no mistaking the action of that horse. . .it was the black stallion.

Mustangers say that nobody but those who have experienced the chase knows the thrill of the first sight of a wild horse. Tilden is excited, and knows a chance like this will never come his way again. As he sits there, hidden by the limbs of the junipers, he makes his plans.

He begins by tying the pack horse to a limb in the shade of a tree and pulling the pack. He rides a large circle around the wild ones, keeping out of sight. When he shows himself, the horses run away in the general direction of the hidden trap.

Tilden slowly keeps the bunch moving up country. By staying

A wild, black stallion rims above the remuda at a roundup camp on the Rocking R Ranch. (circa 1932) — Courtesy Clint and Donna Conradt, all rights reserved.

well behind the mustangs and showing himself occasionally, he is able to make the horses think this is their own idea. Hours pass as the horses meander up the ridge, barely aware of the rider following at such a long distance.

> . . .the most cunning of all animals — a wild stallion; his speed and endurance were incomparable; his scent as keen as those animals that relied wholly upon scent to warn them of danger, and as for sight, . . . no hoofed creature, except for the mountain sheep used to high altitudes, could see as far as a wild horse.
>
> —Zane Grey, *Wildfire*,
> Black's Reader Service Company, New York, 1945
> by arrangement with Harper & Brothers

As he peeks around some trees, Tilden notices the horses are within a hundred yards of the camouflaged entrance to the trap. He prepares to make a run at the mustangs to push them into the wings, but something happens that makes his heart stand still. The stallion slides to a stop, snorts, and stampedes off the ridge into the canyon below.

Tilden rides closer to the band of mares that remain on the ridge. He is worried that the black has left the country. A long, whistling snort from the canyon to his left tells him the stud is waiting for its mares to follow.

Tilden spurs ahead to the right of the mares. They plunge off the ridge toward the stallion as Tilden makes a hair-raising ride into the canyon to the right. Circling the trap, he rides down into the other canyon where the mustangs are milling around.

Tilden jumps the wild ones, then follows as they lunge back up the ridge. His heart is in his throat when the bunch tops out and heads down country away from the trap. Suddenly the black spooks again, and the whole bunch whirls around and races into the entrance. Tilden rushes ahead to the trap, dismounts at a run, and closes the gate.

He then rides over to see what had scared the horses. Another mustanger who wanted the black for himself had burned a pile of dead juniper limbs a hundred yards in front of the entrance. Those burned ashes had scared the black away, and when it looked as if all had been lost, that same streak of ashes had spooked the mustang back up the ridge and into the spreading wings of Tilden's trap.

That night Tilden rides down country to where he had left his pack horse. He repacks the animal and travels to his camp, arriving at daylight. He hobbles his horses on some good grass, fixes breakfast, and strolls over to look at the black stallion.

Tilden is greeted by a loud snort. The mares jam against the posts at the backside of the corral, but the stud remains in the center, challenging the man. With fire in its eyes, its long foretop hanging over them, the fierce stallion stands defiantly. As the mares mill around behind him, he watches and waits for a chance at the human who trapped him.

Tilden changes his mind about walking into the corral to forefoot the black. Instead he climbs the high corral posts and sits there for a couple of minutes thinking things over. Then he takes a couple of half hitches around one of the posts with his rope, shakes out a loop, and flips it over the horse's head.

> Without ever tightening the slack on the loop around its neck, the horse had stood, watching him. Then, all at once, that good-looking head was transformed to look like one of these dragons that's seen in pictures. The glimpse Tilden got of its mouth and eyes and nostrils more than reminded him of one, and the only difference was there was no flame or smoke out of neither the mouth nor nostrils. But the look was sure there, and as that head appeared above the nine foot fence at him, and the weight of its body shook the whole corral, Tilden didn't want to see more. He just made sure he fell off on the outside, and when he hit the ground the front of his shirt was missing.

Illustrations from *Sand*.

"*The weight of his body shook the whole corral.*"

"*A-straddle the black.*"

The bronc stall.

As the stud fights the rope, Tilden runs around and opens the gate. The mares file out at a fast pace, and as the last one departs he glances around and sees the stud choke down and fall over on its side. He hurriedly closes the gate and runs over to loosen the rope from the post. Jumping on the horse's neck, he grabs one ear, holds up its nose and slips on the hackamore. When the stallion struggles upright on shaky legs it is tied solid once more, but this time there is no choking loop. Instead, the rope is run through the bosal and tied around its neck with a non-slip bowline knot.

The fire is burning bright in that horse's eye as Tilden stands there out of breath and out of the stud's reach. He suddenly realizes that this horse is the absolute spirit of wild freedom and he, Tilden, is taking that freedom away from it. Tilden doesn't blame the horse for fighting back. For a fleeting moment he even thinks about turning it loose, but discards that idea because he knows the horse would be hounded again and again by every mustanger and cowboy in the country until it's captured again.

Tilden builds a bronc stall on one side of the corral where the fighting stud horse can be hazed and pulled into the stall, its head tied down, and a rope lashed over its withers. With a timber wedged behind it, the horse can be safely handled inside this contraption. Tilden ties a box to the end of the stall and puts a handful of grain in it. The horse doesn't know what grain is, but one day in anger it accidentally takes a bite and begins to acquire a taste for oats.

When the man first touches the shiny, black hide of the horse, it tries its best to tear the stall apart. Tilden pets the stallion, talks to it, then climbs all over it while the trembling stud is tied down in the stall. He then saddles the trapped horse and sits in the seat of the saddle. Afterwards, he rewards the stallion with a handful of grain. Many weeks later the horse gentles down enough to be handled in the open corral, where Tilden eventually rides it.

Those months of preliminary gentling pay off. The horse doesn't even buck the day Tilden calls on all his nerve to ride the stallion outside. Because of Tilden's gentle handling and the time he takes

202

Will James in the door of the studio where he wrote Sand *in 1929.*

to win the wild horse's confidence, both horse and man build a feeling of trust in each other.

Tilden is mighty proud when he rides the stallion to the cow country below and shows the folks that he has caught the most sought-after horse in that part of the West. At the end of the book the stallion is branded and turned loose with a select bunch of mares, enjoying complete freedom for the remainder of its life.

Tilden's greatest triumph, however, is in overcoming his weaknesses and achieving status as a man. At the beginning of the book he is a drunken sot, an Easterner who exists in a twilight world. He is half a man, despised by all who know him, especially his rich father. When he becomes lost on the Montana prairie he wanders around and eventually stumbles into a cow camp. His exposure to the hard-working cowboys, along with the absence of liquor, starts him rehabilitating himself. He proves-up in the cow country by first proving to himself that he can stand on his own "hind legs".

203

"Tilden goes on to catch another black horse in the civilized, financial world of his father."

Sand is an inspiring book, a book of ideals. It deals with surmounting obstacles and of overcoming human weaknesses. When Bill wrote about Tilden's courage and ability to get off the bottle, he was no doubt trying to give himself the courage to do the same. But Bill couldn't live happily ever after. His life-long dream, the Rocking R, had to be paid for, and this called for him to keep working or lose everything. He wrote a novel a year and visited Hollywood's movie studios regularly in hopes of selling movie rights to his new books. These business pressures and a drinking problem prevented him from living the life he wanted on his dream ranch. His dream was rapidly turning into a nightmare.

An ancient Greek statesman, General Xenophon, who was a student of horse psychology, wrote a book on horsemanship several centuries ago. He believed, "The outside of a horse is good for the inside of a man." If Bill could have physically turned to his strongest forte, the horse, for release from all his pressures, he might have survived such a rapid climb to success. Working all day and night drained his resources, and his mind and body became tired. To keep going, Bill drank continually for stimulation and eventually succumbed to drinking's devastating effects. Bill lost Alice and he lost his dream, the Rocking R.

> *"There is only one true forgiveness; that of understanding what made the other person act as he did, and understanding it so fully that you discover you have nothing to forgive."*
>
> *– Ralph Waldo Emerson*

Bill's lifelong dream was to live on his own ranch where he could work cows and paint pictures of the cowboy and his horse at work. —

WILL JAMES
III-'26
LOOK AT THEM DAGGONE CATTLE, BILL
THEY'VE WALKED RIGHT OVER THE
SNOW DRIFT INTO THE STACK YARD—
THAT'S ALL RIGHT FRED, LEAVE 'EM BE—
TO DAY IS CHRISTMAS.
May this Christmas be merry and
happiness follow on undisturbed
Sincerely
Alice and Bill

Courtesy Clint and Donna Conradt, all rights reserved

To the end of the trail, always a cowboy.

Chapter VIII

ODE TO THE OLD COWMAN

"I'm still riding. It's most all done on canvas and drawing paper, of course, but in doing that I'm living again what I've experienced. When I illustrate a story or write one, the characters and ponies I use are some I've seen and knowed. I don't try to make 'em look pretty no more than I try to better my English. I only try to be natural and put things down as I seen and lived 'em."

Will James, *Nevada State Journal*,
October 26, 1924

207

UNLIKE CHARLIE RUSSELL and Frederick Remington, Will James' popularity declined after his death. His admirers numbered in the millions in the 1920s and 1930s, and no one knows why his popularity faded so rapidly.

In 1942 the world was in the throes of World War II, and perhaps there wasn't time to think about a dead cowboy. Will James told folks one "helluva whopper" in his autobiography; maybe the public resented being fooled by a national hero.

There was also the ever present fact that Bill became an alcoholic and spent his later years drinking excessively. One of his friends described the last days of Will James as tragic days, not days upon which you could build a nice picture of a man. They were especially sad because his early years were marked with genius and many fine qualities.

Whether it was simply love of liquor or the fact that he had to have it as a crutch to hide or drive away something, no one but Bill knew for sure. Whatever the reason, the result was disastrous to him. Will James was a paradox. The lone cowboy's stories had happy endings,

— Special Collections Department, University of Nevada Reno Library.

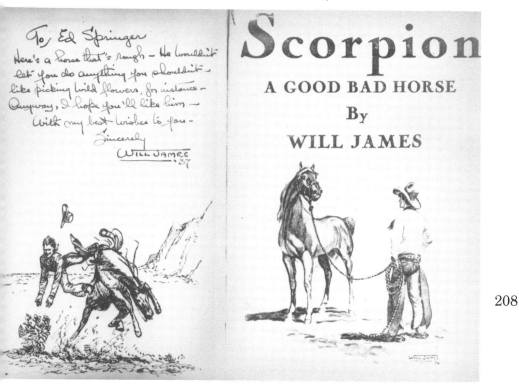

208

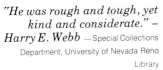

"He was rough and tough, yet kind and considerate." – Harry E. Webb — Special Collections Department, University of Nevada Reno Library

but by some quirk of fate his own life ended in just the opposite way.

In these days of overpopulation, acid rain, toxic waste dumps, and fear of nuclear war, reading a Will James book can be very comforting. There's something peaceful about the thought of a horse camp in the high desert where the most important job of the day is to ride a wild colt and keep a leg on each side of him with your mind in the middle.

There are countless people around who are happy that Bill thought it important to devote his life and his immense talent to portraying range cowboys as he knew them. He illustrated for us with pictures and words what the working days of a cowboy's life were like in the teens of this century. Bill was dedicated to showing folks that the working cowboy's West wasn't as the "shoot-'em-up" novels pictured it.

Not many artists have a photographic mind as Will James had, with total recall. There's a resulting honesty in his drawings. His work is inspiring in that he drew these wonderful illustrations from his mind, his heart, and experience gained through his tailbone during years spent on a horse. Some folks might even label that integrity. The simplicity of drawing a cowboy, often himself, and his 50/50 pardner, his cowpony, doing a day's work with class and style is always present in Bill's work.

Without a doubt the name of 'Will James' has been on more tongues than that of any other cowboy as his books and western stories were of world-wide fame. From the gound up, every inch of this six-foot writer was cowboy, his background was cattle and mustang country, and in later years his books and paintings had the tang of branding hair and the squeal of fighting broncs in every word, for he wrote exactly what he lived. He was rough and tough, yet kind and considerate.

— Harry E. Webb, "Will James and the Rustler,"
Nevada Magazine, 1984, pg. 37

Will James' sentimental dream of the West, a roundup camp on his Rocking R Ranch. This photo hung in the home of Clint Conradt for several decades, where moisture seeped under the glass and wrinkled the corners. (circa 1929)

Wherever he happened to be or whoever he was with, a sober Bill was always his unaffected and unspoiled self, a man of bashful quiet dignity. A drunk Will James showed different characteristics. His doctors advised him that he must quit drinking, for he expressed self-hate and anger when he drank. They warned that his frequent blackouts, not remembering what he had done, could have serious consequences.

During one of his long drinking spells Bill sold his dream ranch, The Rocking R, for a small sum. Alice was notified by her lawyer in Billings to come as soon as possible.

The bill of sale was partially nullified, although the ranch stock and equipment had already been sold by the buyer. Alice filed for a legal separation and received the ranch property, which she sold to pay off all the debts. Bill retained the rights to his published works.

> Success had cost James a tragic price. While it had made him a hero, as the public adores heroes, the astuteness of F. Scott Fitzgerald's 'show me a hero and I will write you a tragedy' fits Will James with mold-like perfection. He had lost Alice, Fred, Dolly, and Clint for whom he had planned to do so much; and gone too was the Rocking R which represented his sentimental dream of the West.
>
> — Anthony Amaral, *Will James, The Gilt Edged Cowboy*,
> Westernlore Press, 1967

Why do so many bowlegged athletes turn into slaves to a bottle of booze? Is it the excitement of having lived every youthful day to its fullest? Is it an aching body that is old and broken before its time and whiskey eases the pain? Is it knowing that youth and vitality are gone and only the memory of those days remain? Or is it simply a yearning for the never-forgotten freedom of the open range?

Cirrhosis of the liver, chronic nephritis, and chronic jaundice killed Will James. Many other "ranahans" in the past have died of these symptoms brought on as a result of daily drinking over many years.

Bill's last few months were spent in an apartment in Hollywood. He completed his final book in March of 1942, *The American Cowboy*. In July, Alice dropped by for a brief visit with the husband she hadn't seen in six years. She was shocked at Bill's appearance. The once handsome, smiling cowboy was reduced to a bag of bones, completely absorbed in his own world.

Bill's secretary and housekeeper cooked food for him, but he couldn't eat. Even watered-down bourbon was bad on an empty stomach. His body was failing fast.

On August 28th, 1942, Bill's legs folded under him, and he was rushed to the Hollywood Presbyterian Hospital. He was able to hold on for a few days.

WILL JAMES, cowboy artist and writer, who died in California He was a native of Great Falls, Mont.

Will James, Author, Dies in Hollywood

HOLLYWOOD, Sept. 3. - (P) - Will James, 50, who years ago left the Montana range lands of his birth and won fame as writer and painter, died at 5:15 a. m. today at Hollywood Presbyterian hospital.

James, author of more than a score of self-illustrated books and uncounted short stories and articles, had been in ill health for months, but entered the hospital only a week ago.

Clipping from a Los Angeles newspaper. (circa 1942)

Even at the end, Bill was strong-willed. He insisted that he wanted his bourbon, and not watered down. He wanted his cigarette "makin's," and he wanted to be out of the hospital so he could go home and "git to work." This was at a time when he was becoming weaker and weaker. He retained a mind of his own about everything, even the covers on his bed and whether he wanted to sit up or lie down. All of this indicated that he never gave up.

At 5:15 in the morning, September 3rd, the Lone Cowboy, whose own advice was to "ride for the High Points," cashed in his chips. He had lived fifty years and three months.

Bill's friend Dick Dickson made arrangements for a famous quartet of that time, The King's Men, to sing "Home on the Range" at the funeral. A small group of friends were there; Dick Dickson, Bill's secretary and a friend, Mrs. Alice James and a few of her friends; Earl Snook of Billings, Shorty Miller, Joe De Yong; and several of the "fellers" who had known Bill.

Bill had directed the executor of his last will and testament to have his body cremated and the ashes scattered over his Rimrock Studio on five acres at the end of Smoky Lane.

Bill came back much in the same manner as two other notable Montana sons, Chief Black Otter and Luther Yellowstone Kelly, who requested they be brought back to the country they loved for burial.

"I feel my body will rest better in Montana," wrote Luther Yellowstone Kelly, frontiersman, scout, soldier of the Indian campaigns, and noted officer of the Spanish-American War, in his will written at Paradise, California. He was given a military funeral and buried on Kelly Mountain outside Billings, Montana, in 1929.

BAY-POO-TAY-SPITA-COT (Black Otter), mortally wounded in 1861, uttered one last request before his departure to the "happy hunting ground." It was his wish to be buried on the rimrock overlooking what was then the domain of his tribe centering along the Yellowstone River.

One hundred and fifty friends and admirers silently watched as

Will James' ashes were released from a circling plane. A long-time friend of his, Reverend Forrest W. Werts of the First Methodist Church of Billings, delivered the following eulogy:

There are souls, like stars, that dwell apart even though in tangency to others by the common pursuits by which fates propinquinize us, and who, because of some special endowment, so stud the sky with stars that others may have visions in the darkest moments of the night.

Of such is Will James. You are here to honor him, while the ashes that once were animated by his animating spirit are scattered to the winds to become a part again of the good earth. You have a common tie with him in your love of saddle leather. His soul has gone to roam the ranges of the eternal, while his art lingers to lead those who love the West toward unforgetfulness. That which he created knows no death, and only as those who come to know the soul of those who conquered the West shall they come to live on in simulation the glory that belongs to those who dared the bronc, endured the hardships, and lived the life of thrilling freedom.

In my youth I knew, personally, Charles M. Russell, the great artist of Northern Montana. He fascinated me with his uniqueness. He too, was an artist, and artist clay is not common mud. His horse was part of him and his bead sash that he wore at his belt was romance to my youthful imagination.

At a Billings, Montana rodeo, Will James proved to "hisself" and to the folks in the stands that he hadn't forgotten how to ride a bucking bronc. He did so by riding his namesake, a horse called Will James. The smile on Alice's face is telling the old boy that he still has what it takes. — Courtesy Clint and Donna Conradt, all rights reserved.

214

Then I came to Billings and met Will James, another painter of the land of my native soil and a writer of even greater dimensions. You see, my early life was tangent to the men of the saddle; those riders of the sage and buckbrush; those wranglers of the cattle herds; those men and women of the yesteryears, who made life for me, beautiful with color. My own father-in-law has been in the saddle in Montana for more than 60 years, and he is one of the finest men I have ever known. It is just the fact that I was born among them - married into one of their families, that these real riders I know, and so speak about Will James.

We pay our tributes never to the one to whom we wish to bear honor. We pay all our tributes to ourselves, always, but we never seem to know it. When someone comes along and puts into poetry or prose; into pen and ink or crayon, or in pigment on a piece of canvas, the words or pictures we'd like to paint - when they have done the things we'd like to do — we pay our homage to them. They epitomize the passions of our own desires, and we reflect in them our own frustrations. We know more about ourselves when we know the folks we glorify for that which they have done.

Will James dramatized the coveted hope of all who would like to endure the tedious and the arduous labors of whipping into shape those contributive forces and factors which make for life's abundancy.

Will James left a heritage of lore; in picture and in printed word, in letters many, sufficient to give color to our time for all time. He painted for us the West with the glory of its sunrise and the beauty of its sunset and lived through the time between without missing the shades and shadows.

No one who loved the ruggedness of real riding, the uncertain seat astride a twisting, pitching bronc, the flow of tail and mane admist the passing winds, the feel of questioned security as hoof beats uncertain sod; the whirl of the rope, the strain of the pull; the thrill of it all and still keep the humor of it; can leave Will James as a phantom rider of the past. So you and I pay tribute to the memory of a man who put down for the future the sagas of our West and left us richer in mind and memory because he was born — an artist, and with that artistry knew all those vicis-

JACK SHIELDS THROWN FROM WILL JAMES

situdes which accompany the realistic living of the life he portrayed.

Some few years ago at the rodeo there was a horse called 'Will James.' You will remember, some of you, that Will James the artist rode out of the chute and through to the whistle on Will James the horse. I sat on the top railing of the chute that day. I saw Will James ride Will James. That Will James that was horse flesh was no less an artist at the bucking business than was Will James the artist of word and brush, astride Will James the artist at pitching, depicted for us that strange something we all realize, sometimes, within our very selves, the duality of our individuality. Our spirits ride our bodies of flesh. And so Will James the artist, rode Will James the genius to turn out an enormous amount of work, in books, in pictures, letters.

And now Will James, that genius, and that artist, who rode Will James, the man, have stopped for the last whistle. The work of the genius lives, on earth and the soul of the man, some do believe, lives on — possibly at eventide new sunsets for the day that is done. And you, who stand to see his ashes float to the earth, look out and beyond the world of things, to the soul that makes things significant, and pay our tribute in our dedications to keep and protect the land wherein such are challenges to the creative artist.

Rev. Forrest W. Wertz, "The Spirit of Will James,"
Billings Gazette, 1947

216

And so, instead of being laid to rest in a hole in the ground like most people, the drifting cowboy's remains were cast to the restless winds, to drift forever over the Montana range lands.

Some of the tiny burned particles sprinkled over the backs of Pecos and Cortez, Bill's last two horses, as the ponies cropped grass nearby. Other particles were swept away skyward and blown toward the foothill country. They settled in a sandy draw, but not for long. A whirling dust devil crossed the draw, and, as it merged the particles with sand and dust, the dervish twisted over a rocky rise and began to disintegrate.

A small bunch of mustangs was bedded down on the lee side of the hill. Some of the ashes sprinkled on the shiny, silky back of a black colt. As it leaped to its feet, head up, nostrils flaring, quivering all over, the little mustang was the very picture of a wild and independent soul.

A horse or a cow that is turned out or escapes into the back country will return to the wild. Are humans so different from other animals? How many of us are tormented with the nagging desire to head to the freedom of the hills and deserts? How often do we feel an insatiable longing for the wild country, to see what lies beyond the next ridge?

Will James was continuously haunted by such invisible forces. If he believed in God, this belief was reflected in his reverence for the wide, lonely desert.

Will James' last saddle displayed with some of his art. —
Special Collections Department, University of Nevada Reno Library.

217

If a monument was ever erected in memory of Will James, surely it would have an inscription not unlike this final stanza from the following old poem:

ODE TO THE OLD COWMAN

When my old soul hunts range and rest
  Beyond the last divide,
Just plant me in some stretch of West
  That's sunny, lone, and wide.
Let cattle rub my tombstone down
  And coyotes mourn their kin
Let hawses paw and tromp the moun'
  But don't you fence it in!

— Author unknown, from the book
Before Barbed Wire
by Mark H. Brown and W. R. Felton,
Bramhall House, New York, 1956

Whitehorse Ranch, Fields, Oregon. — Photo by Kurt Markus © *1987*.

Presenting a selection of five drawings
by the cowboy, Will James.

"With all the rambling I done which was for no reason at all only
to fill the craving of a cowpuncher that always wanted to drift
over that blue ridge ahead, my life was pretty well with my horse
and I found as I covered the country, met different folks, and seen
many towns, that the pin-eared pony under me (which ever one it
was) was a powerful friend, Powerful in confidence and strength.

"A horse got to mean a heap more to me than an animal to carry
me around, he got to be my friend, I went fifty-fifty with him, and
even though some showed fight and I treated 'em a little rough
there'd come a time when we'd have an understanding and we'd
agree that we was both pretty good fellers after all."

221

Pen and ink drawing for **All In A Day's Riding** *(1933)*.

Pencil drawing for **The Drifting Cowboy** *(1929)*.

— Courtesy of Mr. and Mrs. A.P. Hays.

— Copyright © 1929 Charles Scribner's Sons; copyright renewed 1961 Auguste Dufault. Reprinted with the permission of Charles Scribner's Sons.

224

Untitled pencil drawing.
— Courtesy Mr. and Mrs. A.P. Hays.

"Wild Horse Round-Up," pencil drawing for Sun Up *(1931)*.

Glossary

Bosal: from the Spanish *bozal*, meaning muzzle. A bosal is the essential part of a hackamore. It is a braided rawhide noseband developed by the Spanish for training young horses. It applies pressure to the nose and chin and takes the place of a bit for controlling a horse so that the tender bars of a young horse's mouth might not be injured.

The standard bosal measures twelve inches from the inside of the nose button (a long braided knot seven or eight inches in length) to the heel knot. Bosals are braided over a twisted rawhide core with two buttons braided on each side to keep the headstall in place. A large, round heel knot holds the two ends together and adds some weight at this point for a quick release of pressure.

When the horse knows how to work in a bosal he can be double-reined into a bridle with a bit in his mouth. A double-rein rig is used for an advanced stage of training where the horse wears both a bosal with reins and a bridle with bit and reins. He is handled with the bosal and simply carries the bit until he becomes accustomed to it.

Bronc buster: most all large cattle ranches had a bronc buster to start colts for the remuda. They drew only a few extra dollars a month for riding the rough string, but they had the respect of every man on the outfit.

The bronc rider would "hang and rattle." He didn't have time to gentle a horse first but would buck the horse out quickly to save the boss time and money. His calling demanded that he not be bucked off, both as a matter of pride and because horses learned to become outlaws when they could throw their riders.

Buckaroo: a cowboy of the great basin that includes northern Nevada, northern California, eastern Oregon, and western Idaho. The word is a corruption of the Spanish word *vaquero* (cowboy).

The type of horsemanship seen on these ranges goes back directly to the horse-training techniques perfected by the Californios in the 1700s and 1800s. The Californio style of horse jewelry — silver spurs, bits, and conchos — and other Californio-styled horse gear such as saddles and bridles, are used by most buckaroos today, although this equipment is modified for more strength.

The cowboy borrowed his traditional gear from the Spanish as freely as he borrowed from the *vaqueros'* word supply. Western terminology today owes much of its origin to Spanish, however little it resembles the original either in spelling or pronunciation.

232

Buckaroo Saddle: a specially designed saddle for riders who are a-horseback every day. Developed from the Californio saddles, these saddles have narrow forks in the front (slick fork) with bucking rolls added. The narrow forks eliminate the legs being spread and keeps the rider closer to the horse.

These saddles have a high cantle in the rear to support the rider's back, and the cincha is moved toward the center to help the riders balance when an ol' pony "blows the plug." Because a tight cincha will stay at the girthline behind the horse's shoulders, a 5/8, 3/4, or 7/8 rigging keeps the swells over a horse's withers, which is his center of balance. Usually a rear cinch is added to keep the saddle in place while roping.

Caballada: Spanish, pronounced Kab-a-yada. It is the supply of saddle horses maintained by a cattle ranch. Most buckaroos in the Northwest shorten the word to "Cavvy."

Chaps: pronounced shaps, a cowboy abbreviation of the Spanish word *chaparejos*, meaning leather overalls. In Will James' day, bat wings were the popular type of chaps worn by many northern cowboys. They were made of heavy bullhide with wide, flapping wings. They were held on by straps and buckled underneath the flaps. Straps were secured by three to six nickel or silver conchos down each leg. They are worn primarily to protect a rider's legs from injury when he is thrown or when a horse falls on him, pushes against a fence or another animal, attempts to bite him, or carries him through brush, cactus or chaparall. They also provide protection against rain or snow.

Cowboyed-up: proved himself as a rider.

Cutting horse: on a cattle ranch the most specialized horses were always the cutting or sorting horses. It was important for these horses to have a natural aptitude for working cattle, to be self-starters and supple athletes. A cutting horse will walk into a herd of cattle on stealthy feet. When a rider indicates which animal or pair he wants to sort, the horse will drive the cow to the edge of the herd. The cow never wants to leave the herd on open ground and will frantically race back toward the other cattle. The cutting horse blocks all of the cow's efforts to return to the bunch.

Dally and tie-hard man: the age-old argument between the California way of riding and handling stock and the Texas way. The California buckaroo rode a center-fire (one cinch in the middle) rigged saddle, threw a long rope, and took his dallies (from the Spanish, *dar la vuelta*) around the horn. The Texas cowboy carried a short rope tied to the saddle horn. He rode a full double-rigged saddle, one cinch in front directly under the swells and one to the rear of the saddle.

Eared down: To distract a bronc's attention by holding its head down by the ears, allowing another cowboy to saddle or pack the animal.

Ear-soured horses: when a bronc has been eared down a few times to be bridled he gets "mighty perticular" about his ears and won't allow anyone to touch them.

Fiador: from the Spanish, sometimes called theadore. In his book, *Uncle Bill*, Will James describes it as ". . .a doubled cotton rope that ties around the neck and fastens to the bosal under the chin, that's called a 'feador', and in the making of it is two of the most complicated knots a man ever invented." The fiador holds the hackamore in place on a colt's head when ridden the first few times. Once a colt is going good and responding to cues from the rider, a fiador is taken off, allowing the heel knot to drop more rapidly, which allows a faster release of pressure.

Foundered: a horse is foundered by a fever or heat buildup in its body. The horse's hoof is encased in a round, solid shell. The heat inside this shell causes the outside of the hoof, known as the horn, to separate from the sole of the hoof.

Garcia, Guadalupe S. and his wife, Saturnina, came to Elko the day before Thanksgiving in 1896 with two suitcases of spurs, bits, reatas, headstalls, and reins. They set up shop in the lobby of the Gen Hotel owned by Charles Mayer. That same evening Garcia negotiated with Mayer to rent a building on Railroad Street and within a week had nailed up a sign proclaiming he was a harness and saddlemaker. For 36 years he and his superb craftsmen turned out quality gear for stockmen, and he became one of the most famous saddlemakers in the nation.

Born in Sonora, Mexico, he was three years old when his family moved to San Luis Obispo, California. As a youngster he was fascinated with saddlemaking and engraving. When he was 19 he became an apprentice at the Arana shop. Arana was known as a master in the business.

Garcia soon opened his own place in nearby Santa Margarita. As the Garcia name grew in fame, Nevada cowmen began buying from him, and he heard many stories of Elko, a busy cowtown in the northeastern corner of the state. He decided to move to the place.

A brother joined the firm in 1903. His job was to drive a wagon throughout northern Nevada, Idaho, and Oregon selling and taking orders. In that same year Garcia crafted the noted saddle adorned with gold and silver engraving which was displayed and won awards at the 1904 World's Fair in St. Louis. From then on his fame was firmly established, and many dignitaries rode his saddles, including several Nevada governors.

— 1985 Garcia Bit & Spur Company catalog

Gaskin: a muscular area above the hock on a horse's hind leg.

Glass-eyed: a horse with one or two white eyes. The pupil is small and sometimes blue in color.

Grulla: pronounced groo-ya, from the Spanish meaning crane-colored. It is a mouse-colored horse with a black mane and tail and black socks to its knees. Like the dun, some of them have zebra stripes on their legs and even on their necks and shoulders. A dark dorsal stripe two inches wide running from the withers to the tailbone is common. Also called blue-grey, smoky, and mouse dun.

Gullet: a space saddlemakers leave in a saddle directly below the horn at the base of the swells. It's handy for carrying the saddle.

Hackamore: from the Spanish word, *jaquima*, meaning headstall. The complete hackamore includes a bosal, headstall, fiador and McCarty. A headstall 1/2 inch wide attaches to each cheek of the bosal and adjusts so that the nose button will be where the gristle enters the bony part of the horse's nose, making a slant down to the jaw knot of the hackamore.

In the 1700s and 1800s the Californios developed stock-horse training to a fine degree and would keep their horses in a hackamore until the horse knew how to work well; then they would double-rein the colts into a bridle. To save time, today's buckaroos start a colt in a hackamore for the first few rides, then go to a snaffle bit for the remainder of their training. They put the colt back into a hackamore during its fourth year when it is cutting teeth.

Hog-nosed Tapaderos: sometimes shortened to "taps," the word is from the Spanish and means the leather covering of a stirrup. Wrapping around both sides and front, the leather protects the rider's boots from cactus and brush. In northern areas they protect feet from the weather. Hog-nosed taps have two leather conchos in the front above the snout or toe area that give an appearance of a hog's face.

Honda: a braided rawhide eyelet in the business end of a reata for making a loop. As the rope slides through the honda, it closes and becomes a snare. In grass or nylon the honda is tied and reinforced with a leather burner to keep the honda from wearing through.

Hoosegow: from the Spanish *juzgado*, meaning jail.

Hoolihan loop: sometimes called the herd loop, it is the most commonly used rope throw on a ranch. Instead of whirling a rope overhead to build momentum for a throw, the houlihan (or hooley ann) can be cast quietly. When roping horses, the large loop is laid on the ground to the roper's left side. When he spots the horse he wants, the loop is brought forward, circled over his head and turned upside down for the throw. For casting long distances an extra coil is held in the same hand with the loop.

Kept a-hookin' it: riding bucking horses. Spurring and hooking are synonymous.

Lariat rope: from the Spanish *la reata*, meaning to fasten or to catch. It is the cowboy's most useful tool, the catch rope.

Long in the tooth: cowboy vernacular for getting old. A typical cowboy's way of describing a horse's condition when referring to his own. As a horse gets older, its teeth begin to erupt from the gums, and its teeth actually get longer each year.

McCarty: from the Spanish word *mecate*, meaning a twisted horse-hair rope.

McCartys are often black and white in color. Not only are these decorative, they are easy for a horse to see with its peripheral vision. When a hackamore colt is in training, the leading rein is held out to the side for the horse to see. This helps the colt come around faster.

McCartys are usually 22 feet long with a knot in the end that the Spanish call, *la mota*. The knot is placed between the cheeks of the bosal above the heel knot, and wraps are taken around the bosal and pulled tight. A loop of the rope is drawn up between the wraps to form the reins. Most horse trainers prefer the reins to be long enough to wrap around the swells of the saddle. The remaining length of rope is pulled downward through the wraps for a long lead rope. The lead rope is tucked into the belt of the rider's chaps. If the rider is bucked off, he has the lead rope to hold onto so he doesn't have to walk back to camp.

Picket rope: a picket rope is an oversized, soft cotton rope tied to the horse's halter or to a leather strap around the front leg. The other end is tied to a log or a picket pin which has been driven into the ground.

The soft rope doesn't burn the hide off a horse's legs. As they graze around the anchor, horses soon learn how to handle the length of rope.

Quirt: from the Spanish word *cuarta*. A flexible, braided rawhide riding whip with a short stock and two long leather poppers in the small end. A loop is attached to the large end so that it can be carried on the rider's wrist or on the saddle horn. When used to whip a horse, the loop is around the center finger of the rider's right hand. In the old days the stock was sometimes filled with lead to strike down a rearing horse that threatened to fall over backwards.

Ranahan: cowboy terminology often shortened to "ranny," it means a top cowhand.

Reata: Spanish word meaning rope to tie horses. A catch rope made of braided rawhide, rawhide being untanned leather. After the hair and all flesh has been removed from a raw cowhide, it is cut into long thin strings to be braided into ropes and other horse gear.

Rep: a representative from a neighboring ranch. A rep with his own string of horses would trail over and ride along with a roundup as long as it bordered his range. He worked the same as all the other hands, and his stock was branded with his outfit's own brand. After the gather, he trailed 'em all home: a little bunch of cows and calves with a bull or two, his string of saddle horses, and a pack horse with the cowboy's bed lashed to its back.

Rodear: a buckaroo term for holding a herd of cows while a cut is made from it, a corruption of the Californio/Spanish word *rodeo* pronounced ro-day-o. In alta California, in the days of huge open range ranchos and Spanish *Dons*, the functions of a rodeo were more or less the same as those of a roundup. The great herds were gathered and held on chosen rodeo grounds. Then the parting began, the mission stock being driven into one *apertado* (cut herd) and the varying brands into other herds.

Sliding Leather Blind: in the old days, most horses were started when they were full-grown. Their ages could vary anywhere between 5 and 9 years. Most of these horses were out of hot-blooded studs (Steeldust, Thoroughbred and Morgan bloodlines) and cold-blooded mares (mustangs). They had some size to them and had only seen humans maybe once or twice in their lifetimes. They were old enough to be independent in their own ways of thinking and large enough to back it up.

All the instincts of a colt tell it to fight back. Bronc busters found that tying a shirt or bandana around the horse's eyes, shutting off its vision, would usually immobilize the large animal long enough to cinch a saddle on its back. This was refined by some cowboys to a leather band approximately 3"x16". It had slots in each end where the headstall fit. It wore like a browband when not in use but could be slid down over the horse's eyes. After a rider mounted, he could either lean over or pull the bonc's head to one side and pull the blind up, then it was "Powder River, let 'er buck!".

Spade bit horses: found throughout buckaroo country. Their method of making these bridle horses is part of a legacy passed down to today's riders from the Californios.

A spade bit is designed to fill, and it is shaped to fit, a horse's mouth. It has certain weight which helps maintain a horse's headset. The cheeks are wide and usually loose-jawed so that a horse, when nervous, cannot chew on the sides, but retains some freedom of movement. Copper wire triggers, or braces, run from the spoon to the cheeks (copper helps a horse's mouth to remain moist). When the rider picks up the weighted, balanced reins, these triggers warn the horse that a new movement is coming and therefore it is not caught by surprise, which would cause it to throw its head up. A horse that goes around with its head in the air is called a stargazer and is most undesirable.

Only horses that know how to work and how to maintain foot position when being worked in a hackamore or snaffle bit should be bridled with a spade bit.

Randy Steffen wrote — "The flashy, turn-at-a-touch bridle horses of the ancient Californios have always been admired by horsemen in every part of the United States. Many an old-timer Texan, fresh from the *brasada* of his home range, stood back and silently admired the maneuverability of the California cow horses at the end of a long cattle drive from Texas to the sunny land of the Pacific (in the 1800s). While he probably didn't approve of the spade bits in the mouths of these *caballos*, he begrudgingly had to admit to himself that the mounts of the dark-skinned *vaqueros* could throw themselves around after a cow.

California was a land of *manana*. . .the cowboys of the *Dons* took many more pains, and much more time, in the training of their bridle horses than the bowlegged knight of the Texas brush country ever dreamed of spending on the Spanish ponies that helped trail herds of Texas cattle to the grassy slopes of the Pacific. But he did admire the results, and would have been proud to own such a mount!"

The Hackamore Reinsman, Ed Connell,
The Longhorn Press, 1952

The Strawberry Roan: by Curley Fletcher, can be found in dozens of books of representative American folk music and on early phonograph records. One of the best known recordings is on Marty Robbin's album of Gunfighter Ballads. The song can always be heard in any cow camp which harbers a guitar picker.

In the early 1930's Ken Maynard sang the tune in a Universal movie called *Strawberry Roan*. In 1931 Everett Cheetham did the song on stage in a New York play entitled *Green Grow The Lilacs*. The play was the forerunner of the musical *Oklahoma*. The tale of the famous roan bucking horse was included in the accompanying booklet with no credit given to the author.

By 1930 the song had become quite famous, but Curley realized little profit or recognition for his work. The song was distributed widely by word of mouth before it was published by a music house with that all important copyright notice attached.

The poem first appeared in a Globe, Arizona newspaper called *The Arizona Record* in 1915. It was printed in the *Century* magazine in 1925 and later that year in *The Nation* magazine.

The song was aired in Phoenix, Arizona by Romaine Lowdermilk and a musical group called The Arizona Wranglers over the local radio station KTAR. They sang the ballad repeatedly to an appreciative audience. Lowdermilk related that he had obtained the song in the early twenties from a singing cowboy named Mark Tracy. Tracy was killed afterwards by a fall from a bronc while riding for the Hayes Cattle Company at Yarnell, Arizona.

Above all, Lowdermilk treasured a copy of Curley's collected poems, *Songs Of The Sage* (1931), whose flyleaf is inscribed with Curley's handwriting: "To my friend Romaine Lowdermilk who is responsible for the popularity of my old Strawberry Roan."

Thoroughbred, Steeldust, or Morgan bloodlines: it was common practice of the open range to turn hot-blooded studs loose on the range to breed mustang mares. Their offspring were often good cowhorses with speed and size. Most legendary horses of the past were such crosses.

The thoroughbred was the long-range race horse of the eastern U.S. and England.

Steeldust was one of the foundation quarter horse sires in south Texas during the mid-1800s. The horse weighed 1,200 pounds and stood over 15 hands tall (a hand measures 4 inches). He passed on his muscling and speed to all his offsrping.

The Morgan horses were lightweight coach horses that originated in Vermont. They were also excellent riding animals. These horses were descendants of a short, prepotent sire of the late 1700s and early 1800s — Justin Morgan.

Tripping a steer: in the open range days, a bunch-quitting steer had to have his bluff called or he couldn't be held in the herd. A rider would spur up to the steer's left side, rope him by the horns and throw the slack in his rope over the steer's rump. He would rein his horse to the left, and the steer would be busted flat on its side as the rope pulled its legs out from under it. The horse held the rope tight as the cowboy ran to the steer and tied its legs together.

Vent a brand: to cancel it with a blockout brand, such as a slash over the top.

War knot: early-day buckaroos and *vaqueros* of the Californio period were proud of the long manes and tails of their mounts and never trimmed them back. When working their horses they often tied the tails in "war knots" to keep the long hair out of the way.

Index